GETTING INTO PRACTICE

Edward Vernon

ISBN: 9781898146292

First published 1979 by
Macmillan London Limited

Also by the same author:
Practice Makes Perfect
Practise What You Preach

Chapter One

The human body can lose a lung, a kidney, half a stomach, several feet of intestine, four-fifths of the pancreas, three quarters of the liver and two pints of blood and still function normally. Modern engineers may feel proud of the fail-safe mechanisms they build into their machines, and may boast about the back-up systems and reserves of power which their designs incorporate, but few man-made machines can match the human body. What other delicate systems operate so effectively in such extremes of temperature, humidity and gravitational pressure? What other piece of sophisticated machinery will continue working more or less normally with its external appearance altered almost beyond recognition and its constituent parts battered, reorganised and partly destroyed?

Of course, even the human body has its limits. There is a point when damage becomes too great for the system to bear and injured parts threaten the viability of the whole.

The motor-cyclist, still lying on the trolley upon which the ambulance crew had wheeled him into the casualty department, had been part of the way across the line which divides the living from the dying when he had arrived at the hospital. In the three or four minutes since then it had become clear to everyone that the crossing was nearly complete.

The duty casualty surgeon, Martin Crisp, needed no such reminders. Short, red-haired and looking younger even than his twenty-five years, Dr Crisp was concerned less with the physiological miracles which had kept his patient alive than with the fact that without a few more miracles he was unlikely to remain alive for very much longer. And there was not only the motor-cyclist to be dealt with; the casualty department was crowded with the injured and the ill, and their relatives and friends. Even at two o'clock on a Sunday morning a city-centre hospital can rely on getting plenty of business.

Dr Crisp had been on duty for eighteen hours, and for the last eight he'd been on his own. Theoretically he was able to call on another junior doctor to help him if things got too busy; in practice no one ever took advantage of the arrangement. The other doctors sleeping in the hospital had been working all night when Dr Crisp had come on duty, and in six hours' time they would again start a twenty-four-hour shift.

I was the only other figure in casualty wearing a white coat, and, although it may have seemed that I was destined to play some active role in the night's continuing drama, the truth was that most of the patients probably knew far more about what was going on than I did. This was my first rich raw taste of clinical medicine, my first experience of real live patients. And, amidst the noise, the cries, the screams, the complaints and the moanings, I felt frozen inside a shell of fear and awe. Frozen stiff and uncertain, like a hare caught midway across a country road in the headlights of an oncoming car.

Dr Crisp had been examining the abdomen of a seven-year-old boy with suspected appendicitis when the motor-cyclist had been brought in. The boy had been in pain for several days, but Crisp decided there was no need to wake the surgeon and have the operating-theatre opened up. He scribbled a note on the boy's admission record and left instructions for his temperature to be taken and his pulse counted in an hour's time.

The motor-cyclist had been in collision with an electricity sub-station. The policeman who had accompanied the ambulance to the hospital, reported that, since the sub-station was some fifteen feet from the road when the cyclist had collided with it, and since no other vehicles were involved, it was his belief that the cyclist had been under the influence of alcohol when the accident had occurred. He was now waiting ghoulishly to try to persuade Dr Crisp to allow him to catch a few of the injured rider's precious and irregular exhalations in his breathalyser bag. Dr Crisp had pointed out that, whatever happened, the motor-cyclist wouldn't be riding or driving any sort of vehicle for at least six months, so that he felt it unlikely that permission would be granted for any official investigations. Those weren't his exact words, but under the circumstances his remarks were perhaps excusable. The policeman, unmoved, stayed where he was.

For the past five hours I'd stood and watched as Dr Crisp had dealt with a fifteen-year-old girl who had taken an overdose of her mother's arthritis pills, a sixty-four-year-old man who'd had a heart attack while playing dominoes in a working-men's club, a middle-aged woman who'd been knocked over by a cyclist and had cut her leg, a four-year-old boy who'd fallen out of a bedroom window and fractured his skull, a twenty-eight-year-old man who'd been given a black eye and a nose-bleed in a fight, a two-year-old with colic, a seventy-three-year-old man with a sprained arm, a woman having a miscarriage, a boy with mumps, a boy with a headless drawing-pin stuck in his bottom, an old man with chest pains, a baby girl with a half-sucked sweet stuck in her ear, and an assortment of other patients bringing with them a good variety of ailments, both real and imaginary. The old man with chest pains and the sixty-four-year-old domino player had both died. The rest had been either treated and sent home or admitted to hospital and bedded down for the night. Now Dr Crisp had the boy with abdominal pains, the motor-cyclist, the boy's semi-hysterical mother, a fourteen-year-old girl with a graze on her forehead, a drunk with a black eye, a woman with swollen ankles and considerable difficulty in getting her breath, and an old man with wax in his ears to deal with. The motor-cyclist, unconscious, bleeding and hardly recognisable, had all his attention for the moment.

My sense of complete and utter uselessness was matched only by my admiration for Dr Crisp. I had no idea how he kept going, let alone managed to make diagnoses and prescribe treatments, in the midst of such confusion. I'd rather have tried to thread a needle on a roller-coaster. At that moment I wished I'd elected to study law, architecture, French literature in the seventeenth century, or sewage disposal — anything, in fact, other than medicine.

He'd put a drip in the motor-cyclist's arm and begun pouring fluids into the collapsed and drained circulatory system; he'd taken blood samples to determine the blood group, in preparation for a transfusion; and he'd already discovered that the patient had a fractured femur, a fractured pelvis, several fractured ribs, probably a ruptured spleen, some internal cerebral bleeding and multiple superficial cuts and abrasions. He'd telephoned for an anaesthetist and a neurosurgeon, and had asked for the radiographer to be called into the hospital to take X-rays which would help him tell just how many other bones were broken. The radiographer, who'd been into the hospital twice already that night, was at home two miles away and would take ten minutes or so to arrive. The anaesthetist lived in the doctors' quarters and would be in the casualty department within half that time. The neurosurgeon, needed to make burr holes in the patient's skull and drain out blood threatening to do permanent damage to his brain, lived thirty-five miles away and would take about an hour. It was Dr Crisp's job to keep the patient alive long enough for them all to arrive. The neurosurgeon, a cautious, pessimistic man, would telephone three times on the way to the hospital to see if his journey was still necessary.

I hadn't seen the woman with the raffia basket come in, and I jumped when she tapped me on the shoulder.

'I wonder if you'd mind giving me a prescription for this.' She took from her pocket a piece of stained material which she held under my nose. It didn't smell too good.

'It's a discharge,' she explained. 'I've had it for a month.' She turned the material over so that I could examine the other side. 'I knew you wouldn't have time to examine me.' She bent a little closer and whispered, 'And I'm a bit shy anyway.'

'I'm not a doctor,' I told her. 'You'll have to go and see your own doctor on Monday.'

'He's never there. Just give me something for it.' She folded up the piece of material and put it back into her pocket.

'I don't know what it is,' I said.

'It's the gusset out of my pants.'

'The discharge,' I said. 'I don't know what that is.'

'Nasty,' she said. 'Very nasty.'

'You'll have to take it to your own doctor on Monday morning,' I told her firmly.

She swore loudly. Clutching her basket she stalked indignantly out of the casualty department. As she disappeared I shrank closer to the wall, in an attempt to disappear completely from view. It was all like some outrageous nightmare. The noise, the speed, the confusion and the smells never seemed to stop. There was no reason for me to stay. I'd gone there simply because I wanted to see what it was like. I had no role to play. I didn't even have to attend as a spectator. But I couldn't leave. It horrified me, but it hypnotised me.

This was my life. This was the way I'd chosen to spend the years stretching in front of me. And it was nothing like the medicine I'd dreamt of; nothing like the medicine I'd seen practised by our family general practitioner; nothing like the medicine I'd dreamt about practising; and nothing like the medicine I'd expected to meet as I'd struggled through the two long years of pre-clinical training. It was real and yet unreal, true and yet not possible. I watched without seeing as the young boy with abdominal pain vomited straight across the policeman's shoes. It was happening a million miles away from me and I was no part of it all.

Suddenly there was a cry from the young nurse who'd been given the task of keeping an eye on the motor-cyclist while Dr Crisp completed his telephone calls.

'What is it?' asked Dr Crisp. He put his hand over the mouthpiece and turned round to look.

The nurse, no more than eighteen-years-old, said nothing. She'd paled, and looked as though she needed to hold on to the trolley in order to stand upright.

'Quick as you can,' murmured Dr Crisp, taking his hand away from the telephone, listening for a moment and then throwing the receiver carelessly back on to the rest. He strode quickly across to the trolley and peered over at the motor-cyclist. I strode timidly forward a yard or two, trying to mirror the casualty doctor's unhurried style. The motor-cyclist had stopped breathing.

'Cardiac arrest,' called Dr Crisp over his shoulder. He leant across and thumped the rider on the chest with unexpected ferocity. The mother of the small boy with abdominal pain screamed and the girl with the grazed forehead fainted, sinking gracefully to the ground. The policeman edged nervously towards her but was beaten to it by the old man with wax in his ears, who carefully straightened out her dress and pushed his folded raincoat underneath her head. The young nurse abandoned Dr Crisp, the motor-cyclist and the trolley and disappeared into sister's office; moments later she reappeared with the casualty sister. Thirty-something, single, forbidding and with a reputation for efficiency, the casualty sister had a sheaf of papers in her left hand and a ballpoint pen in her right. Even casualty medicine involves a good deal of administration. She handed the forms and the pen to the young nurse and moved forward to Dr Crisp. The trolley's brakes weren't working properly and each time Dr Crisp thumped the man's chest the trolley slid away from him.

'Come here,' called the sister, catching sight of me. More frightened of her than of the drama around the motor-cyclist, I hurried forward.

'Take his feet,' she ordered, 'and watch the drip.'

I obeyed, and the three of us lifted him off the trolley and laid him down on the floor. The tube from the drip-bottle only just reached that far and was stretched taut.

'Where's the defibrillator?' asked Dr Crisp.

'On Wellington Ward,' said the sister. 'Two porters are bringing it up when they have a moment.'

'Tea-time, I suppose,' said Dr Crisp drily. He was still banging at the man's chest with his closed fist. The motor-cyclist now had a tube down his throat and the sister was squeezing a black rubber bag. I had no idea how the tube had got there or what the black rubber bag was for. I was terrified of getting in someone's way.

'I hear Mike Entwhistle's passed his fellowship,' said the sister.

'Must be giving it away with cornflakes this year,' said

Dr Crisp. 'I don't reckon much to this poor bugger's chances.'

'He's marrying Helen Warburton.'

'I thought they were married already. They've been living together long enough.'

'We could do with another monitor in case,' said the sister. 'They've had ours in the unit for two days now.'

'There's one on the defib trolley, isn't there?'

'If it's got a plug on.'

'Don't kneel in that sick,' warned Dr Crisp. He was too late; the sister, who'd knelt in the corner of the young boy's vomit, flicked distastefully at the hem of her dress.

The defibrillator and monitor arrived on a small trolley pushed by two lethargic porters. 'Somebody order this?' asked one of them.

'Plug it in,' said Dr Crisp. He paused for a moment and felt the motor-cyclist's wrist. He looked at the casualty sister and shook his head. Turning round he took two paddles which looked rather like table-tennis bats off the trolley. He was smearing them with grease when a tall bespectacled woman in a white coat and the remains of a bouffant hairstyle hurried into the arena. Her coat was fastened only at the top and bottom, and in between could be seen a pale blue nylon nightdress.

'He arrested a couple of minutes ago,' explained Dr Crisp.

'I'm waiting for the neurosurgeon. Motor-cyclist. He's in a bit of a mess.'

'You can save the electricity,' said the newcomer, shining a thin pencil torch into the patient's eyes.

Dr Crisp paused with the paddles held an inch or two above the motor-cyclist's chest.

The woman put her torch back into the top pocket of her white coat and hurried off. Behind her there lingered a haunting smell of horse chestnuts. Dr Crisp tossed the Vaseline-laden paddles back on to the trolley and moved away from the motor-cyclist. Then, changing his mind, he picked them up again and, holding one in each hand, leant over the patient. 'Stand back,' he shouted. He held the paddles against the man’s chest. Nothing happened.

‘It hasn’t got the right plug on it,’ said the sister. ‘It’s not switched on.’

‘Oh shit,’ said Dr Crisp. ‘Let’s have a cup of coffee.’

He turned away from the motor-cyclist and began to move towards the office. ‘Do you know what his name was?’ he asked the sister. ‘I’d better write something on his notes.’

Chapter Two

I remember very little of my first two years at medical school. They were dull preparatory years, crowded with theory and facts, with lists of arteries, veins and nerves, and with bone-dry descriptions of the human skeletal system. There were some memorable moments which signified my progress from schoolboy to student. There was the time when I first entered the medical-school dissecting-room and saw and smelt the rows of preserved bodies awaiting our brand-new scalpels. And there was the day when I first saw my name on the noticeboard where there were pinned lists of students successful in the examinations which marked the dividing-point between pre-clinical students, confined to the study of dead bodies, preserved organs and chemicals in test-tubes, and clinical students, allowed to mix with, talk to and even touch real patients. That was the moment when I first became aware of the fact that I was on my way to becoming a doctor. And it was then, rather than when I first entered medical school, that I first began to understand that the metamorphosis from student to doctor, from human being to medicine-man, is a painful and enervating business; that it's not simply a series of rugby matches, noisy parties and imaginative pranks, and that it involves despair, frustration and heartache more than the enjoyment of draught beer and permissive nurses.

But the landmarks were relatively few. The long hours spent poring over anatomy textbooks and brightly illustrated maps of the human body are now no more than a blurred memory. That first night in the casualty department, however, is etched on my memory as if on steel. Among my convictions there is none that could be described as religious, but by morning I felt myself in need more of spiritual support than technical knowledge.

Those memorable hours came at the end of my very first week as a clinical student. It was early autumn when I'd returned to the medical school after my last long summer holiday. I'd spent the first half of it driving a delivery van for a grocer and the second half spending the money I had earned. Five days in Paris and then twelve in the Italian sunshine had done little to prepare me for life as an embryonic healer.

First there was the equipment to be bought. Within forty minutes I had acquired two smart white coats, a plastic name-badge with EDWARD VERNON stamped on it in black, a brand-new plastic stethoscope lying on a polystyrene bed in a smart blue and white cardboard box, an ophthalmoscope in a grey plastic box, a black plastic patella-hammer and a pencil torch with a clip. It was all rather like acquiring a 'doctor kit' and, although none of us knew how to use the equipment we had bought, we nevertheless displayed it all in our white coat pockets with considerable skill, the stethoscope dangling from one large pocket and the patella-hammer and ophthalmoscope standing upright in the other. Suddenly we really felt like medical students.

At our first lecture we were all told to remove our shirts. Female medical students were not exempt, although none removed more private garments. In those days no girl went without a bra if she had anything to put in one. Then we divided into pairs and listened to each other's heart. Or at least we tried to listen to each other's heart. It must have been a comical sight. Fifty yards of plastic tubing connecting fifty pairs of chests, and a hundred pairs of ears straining to gather in the sounds of a hundred thumping hearts.

The next lesson was even more traumatic. We were all issued with short lengths of rubber tubing, syringes, needles, balls of cotton wool and small glass bottles. Several huge bottles of methylated spirit were placed on tables around the room. And then we were told to take blood from each other. At that moment there must have been at least ninety future surgeons and physicians who'd willingly have picked up their shirts and run had they not been more frightened of the clinical lecturer than of the needles. The fellow with whom I'd found myself paired for the first part of the exercise stared at me with a mixture of fear and revulsion. I stared back at him with similarly mixed emotions. We had to attack each other in cold blood, if you will pardon the expression, and move five millilitres of blood from the warm and comfortable veins in which it flowed to the glass bottle with which we'd been provided. The experiment was intended to teach us something of the rudiments of blood-letting, but it had a more practical purpose. The medical school wished to make sure that all students entering the final three years of the course were fit and able to continue their studies. I thought at the time that they were reluctant to allow anyone not in perfect health to enter such an exhausting profession. With the more cynical but more practical eye of age I now believe they simply wanted to ensure they didn't waste time and money training students not fit enough to last the course.

Tying one of the lengths of red rubber tubing around his own upper arm, the lecturer demonstrated the existence of fat, rich veins in what we knew to be the antecubital fossa. With a calmness and true scientific detachment which mesmerised us, he then pushed a needle into the largest and most pregnant-looking vein and withdrew half a syringeful of blood. It was an awesome sight. Three potential doctors fainted. Today one of them is a successful registrar in general surgery.

At first I could hardly believe his claim that taking blood is sometimes much harder than it looks. After all, all of us have over a gallon of it sloshing around inside us, and you'd think that some of it would be glad of a chance to get away. I know that, if I just nick myself with a razor when shaving, the stuff is lapping around my ankles before I know where I am. Oddly enough, however, the lecturer insisted that getting blood out of some people is rather like getting orange juice out of a lemon.

He explained that it's important to be able to tell the difference between a vein, an artery and a nerve because, If you hit an artery, someone may be injured by the plunger of the syringe as it whistles across the ward and, if you hit a nerve, the court-case may coincide with your holiday.

'If the blood which fills your syringe is bright red,' he warned us, 'you've probably hit an artery, and I suggest you whistle nonchalantly and stick your finger on the place where the bruise is going to be. If you hit a nerve the patient will let you know. And get your sample-bottle ready,' he pleaded. 'There's nothing more embarrassing than filling your syringe and having nowhere to put the blood.' He also told us that, if the patient is ordered to keep his arm folded up, the bruise which he can show his relatives will be considerably smaller than it might otherwise have been.

And, with this far too brief introduction, we were freed to attack each other.

Three times my partner tried to remove blood from my arm. Three times he failed. And I began to wish that I possessed a surname which had not coupled me with such a brutal and unskilled surgeon. Moreover, I never got a chance to practise my own skills on him; with my needle still a yard away from its target, he fainted.

By the time he'd recovered we were all busy wielding our small plastic hammers and hitting each other in the most extraordinary places. There are reflexes to be obtained in the ankle as well as the knee, in the arms as well as the legs. There's even a reflex to be obtained from the nose. And the other end of the hammer, sharpened to a pencil-point, can be used to elicit reflexes from the abdominal muscles and the feet. The human body, as we quickly learnt, is a veritable library of programmed movements, and the absence of one or the heightening of another will enable the skilled clinician to arrive at a diagnosis. Not, of course, that we knew what we were doing. We might just as well have been tickling each other with ostrich feathers.

We peered into the depths of each other's eyes and ears, prodded each other's abdomen in search of kidneys and spleens, counted each other's ribs, waved fingers before each other's eyes and tested hearing by listening to each other's watch ticking. We took each other's blood-pressure, examined each other's eyesight and gazed unhappily down each other's throat. We listened to the sound of air rushing in and out of chests, measured pulses and measured them again after ten minutes' hectic exercise, got each other to touch his toes and even looked up each other's nose. After two days we had at least learnt a great deal about each other, even if we hadn't learnt enough about the human body. The natural human reluctance to touch another person intimately without any sexual overtones had been at least partially overcome. For most of us it was the first time we had touched the naked torso of a member of the same sex. There is more to a medical education than learning the physiology of the liver or the anatomy of the skull.

* * *

At the end of the first week we had still not seen a genuine patient upon whom we could practise our newly acquired skills. We'd been teased and tempted and were now ready for some real clinical medicine. Or so we thought. Eager for a real chance to test our knowledge, several of us drifted into the casualty department, the least formal part of the hospital, where we secretly hoped we might get a chance to save a life — or at least listen to a real chest.

Hector Melton was the first person I knew to spend an hour or two in the casualty department. A competent, neat and systematic student, he had an advantage over many of us: his father was a doctor who had qualified at St Peter's some twenty years before. As a result Hector had contacts. A consultant anaesthetist introduced him to one of the casualty doctors and, while the rest of us were trying to decide where to pin our name-badges, Hector was taking blood samples from casualty victims and, so he claimed, suturing some of the smaller wounds.

I knew him for the simple but important reason that he and I and a third student, Andrew Clay, shared a flat. I knew both of them already when I came back from Italy, of course, but our relationship was tenuous, to say the least. We came together in that accidental way that so often produces the most lasting friendships. We all happened to be in the medical-school corridor at the same time, looking for a flat to rent, when a final-year student about to leave St Peter's for ever arrived with a notice for the students' board. It advertised a flat for three no more than half a mile from the hospital and medical school. The three of us combined to rent it less than five minutes later.

While Hector was short and tidy, Andrew was huge and shaggy. Hector wore dark-blue or grey suits; Andrew preferred brown corduroy trousers and elderly sports jackets. Hector favoured his old school tie; while Andrew always seemed to wear the same brown knit with a toothpaste stain two inches from the bottom. Hector had no obvious vices; Andrew smoked a pipe and had an unpopular habit of showering his immediate neighbours with small, wet, sticky pieces of tobacco while he struggled to get it going. The arrival of a cloud of smoke was usually treated with relief; it did at least mean a respite from the probing and poking.

It was at Hector's suggestion that I'd found myself in the casualty department late on Saturday night. But unlike him I'd arrived unannounced and unheralded. And unlike Hector I'd found my first experience of clinical medicine frightening and forbidding. I'd felt as comfortable there as an agoraphobic at a picnic, and I had just about as much inclination to repeat the experience.

Chapter Three

After a week's basic course on the art of doctoring we were launched upon a public which, while not unsuspecting, was nonetheless generous. St Peter's Medical School was founded in the late nineteenth century and consists not only of the medical-school building itself, an ugly pot-pourri of nineteenth-century vulgar red brick and twentieth-century functional concrete, linked spiritually if not physically to the local university, but also of St Peter's Hospital itself and a variety of other smaller, specialist hospitals such as the maternity hospital, the skin hospital, the mental hospital and the orthopaedic hospital.

Since the damage and chaos which medical students can produce is directly proportional to the number of them in any one place at any one time we were divided into ten roughly equal small groups. Each band of students would eventually spend time in every department of the attached hospitals, but Hector, Andrew and I found ourselves together in the same group of ten, allocated for the first three months to the medical department, where we would be walking the wards.

At five minutes to nine on Monday morning, white coats spotless and neatly buttoned, stethoscopes at the ready and hair neatly combed for our first public appearance, we came together nervously in the corridor outside Parkins Ward, where two sisters and a dozen or so nurses looked after twenty-six female medical patients. We stood in two groups of five, with our backs against the wall, trying to keep out of the way and hardly daring to whisper. Everyone who hurried past us into the ward seemed to be hurrying with great purpose and authority; even the most junior nurses passed with a great rustling of starched uniform and never so much as a glance in our direction.

It was twenty minutes past nine when Dr Grainger, the Professor of Medicine, and his small entourage arrived on the ward. I'd already heard a great deal about him. He'd made a tremendous name for himself in his early thirties when his research had led to the development and perfection of a new form of treatment for relapsing fever, a rare tropical disease caused by insect-borne organisms. By the time Dr Grainger's therapy had been shown to produce tumours in half of the patients who took it, he himself had been awarded numerous international honours and appointed to the professorship at St Peter's. Abandoning research, he had then concentrated on building for himself a reputation as an authority on virus infections. Since there are few known effective methods of treating these, he had ample opportunity to advertise his expertise without fear of contradiction. The author of two textbooks and, with the practical help of his junior staff, several dozen papers and articles in the more esoteric medical journals, Professor Grainger had acquired a reputation which led to his being invited to speak at conferences and meetings all over the world. In addition he often spoke at more public functions, and inevitably he was a regular performer on television. His neat red carnation and gleaming bald head were regular sights in the living-rooms of England.

Professor Grainger's senior assistant, the senior medical registrar, was Claude Taylor, a middle-aged physician anxiously waiting in the wings for something to happen to his superior. Dr Taylor, heavily freckled, always elegant, and precise and pernickety as a vegetarian with an ulcer can be, was the true author of most of the papers and articles which appeared under Professor Grainger's name. He'd acquired a slight reputation as a specialist in the treatment of budgerigar-fancier's lung, but had in recent months begun work on the treatment of angina. This onslaught on a disease which affected millions of potential patients had been inspired partly if not totally by a grant from one of the world's major pharmaceutical companies.

The second member of Professor Grainger's entourage, Dr Wilhemina Tarrant, was beginning her first hospital job as a fully qualified doctor. She'd completed her clinical studies just as we'd finished our pre-clinical studies. There had been a considerable amount of competition for the job of house physician to the Professor of Medicine, and Dr Tarrant had obtained the post as a result of her dedication and reliable clinical record. Coincidentally her father was medical director of the company which had provided the grant for Dr Taylor's new research project. He had also been a contemporary of Professor Grainger.

The Professor's arrival on the ward was the signal for considerable activity in the sister's office. Within moments the corridor was packed with nurses and physiotherapists, dieticians and social workers. All of whom gathered round the Professor clutching sheaves of notes and small cardboard folders. The ward sister, Sister Henderson, supervised the loading of a trolley packed tight with medical notes for all the patients on the ward. A junior nurse, rather red-faced and nervous with the responsibility, was given the task of actually pushing it.

And then there we were, gathered in a tightly packed crowd around an actual patient. After the frenetic chaos of the casualty department there was pleasing order to the medical ward and the professorial ward-round. The beds were neatly made, the bottles of orange squash neatly lined up on bedside lockers, the water-jugs full and the patients' temperature-charts inked in and hung with precision at the bottom of each bed.

* * *

She was eighty, but looked younger, and so frail and small that she seemed lost in the vast whiteness of her bed. Her skin was pale and wrinkled, and her hair thin and almost pure white. On her bedside table an old-fashioned alarm clock ticked away and in front of it a black and white photograph of a young man in the uniform of a private stood on guard.

This is Mrs Kennedy,' said Professor Grainger, with an ingratiating smile of introduction. He peered round at us, allowing his eyes to rest on each one for a brief moment, taking in our plastic name-badges and nodding slightly as he did so.

'Mr Melton,' he said suddenly, swivelling back to face my flat-mate, 'would you be kind enough to find out for us precisely why Mrs Kennedy is occupying one of our extremely expensive hospital beds?'

Hector immediately unsheathed his stethoscope and took a step forward.

'Before you attack poor Mrs Kennedy,' interrupted the Professor as Hector asked the old lady to unbutton her nightdress, 'you might find it helpful to ask her a few questions. The history the patient gives you will often lead you towards a diagnosis before you even lay a hand on her.'

'Er...' mumbled Hector, 'can you tell me what is wrong with you?'

Mrs Kennedy looked up at Professor Grainger.

'Mrs Kennedy is waiting for you to tell her what is wrong with her,' said the Professor drily.

'Have you had a cough?' asked Hector, his face now bright red with embarrassment and confusion.

Mrs Kennedy shook her head.

'Have you been sick?'

'Not since last Christmas when I had rather too much pudding,' said the old lady semi-confidentially.

'Do you get short of breath?'

Mrs Kennedy shook her head.

'Have you got any pain?'

Again the answer was negative.

'Do you get any trouble with your back passage?' asked Hector, clearly having abandoned all hope of making any real headway and taking advantage of the fact that the majority of women over the age of fifty complain about their bowels and will readily discuss their disorders at the drop of an opening remark.

Mrs Kennedy looked puzzled for a moment, then she nodded.

Pleased with himself, Hector turned round to look for a smile of encouragement from the Professor. There wasn't one.

'It's always blocked,' said Mrs Kennedy.

It looked as though Hector had found the right question.

'I don't quite understand why you want to know about it,' said Mrs Kennedy.

'It will help us a great deal,' said Hector warmly.

'It's the boy next door,' said the old lady. 'He always

leaves his bicycle in it.'

There were several stifled sniggers from the outer areas of the audience and Hector nervously rubbed at his chin with his right hand.

'Thank you, Mr Melton,' said Professor Grainger. 'You have a good deal to learn, but do not be discouraged.' He reached forward and took the old lady's hand. 'Would you allow one of these young men to examine you?' He held her hand close to his chest as though she were an elderly relative with a large fortune.

Mrs Kennedy nodded her permission and gazed at him with admiration. This time the professorial eye remained on me.

'Would you listen to Mrs Kennedy's heart for us, Mr Vernon,' said the Professor, 'and tell us what you hear?'

With my own heart thumping away as if desperate to escape, I edged slowly forward. When I pulled at my stethoscope to remove it from my coat pocket, it caught on the notebook I had acquired and in which I intended to jot down all the words of advice I gleaned from my teachers. Mumbling apologies, I picked up the notebook and moved towards the patient. Mrs Kennedy had already unfastened her nightdress and exposed her bony chest to the many pairs of eyes. Her breast tissue had long since disappeared and their existence was remembered by two small brown nipples. Except during amatory fumblings this was the first live, naked female chest I had ever seen. Fingers shaking with fear, I pushed the ear-pieces of my stethoscope into position, checked to make sure that I had the right end of the stethoscope switched on and held the terminal diaphragm to Mrs Kennedy's bony chest.

Instead of the comfortingly repetitive lub-dup lub-dup I had heard when listening to my partner a few days before, I could hear nothing. Nothing, that is, except for the steady tick-tock of the alarm clock on Mrs Kennedy's bedside table. The more I tried to erase the clock's ticking from my consciousness the more I became aware of its existence. The more I strained to hear the beating of her heart, the more I heard the alarm clock. I felt the beads of sweat forming on my brow.

'Identify the first heart sound,' said Professor Grainger kindly, tapping me on the shoulder to attract my attention, 'the sound of the mitral and tricuspid valves closing,' he reminded me, 'and then listen for the second heart sound produced by the closing of the aortic and pulmonary valves.'

I put my stethoscope back into position and leant forwards again. Normally the heart is situated so that the sounds it makes can best be heard roughly in the middle of the left side of the patient's chest.

'Listen for the opening snap of the mitral valve and for the third and fourth heart sounds. Then you can concentrate on the systolic and diastolic murmurs,' went on Professor Grainger.

Once again I replaced my stethoscope and closed my eyes to concentrate on the sound of Mrs Kennedy's heart going about its normal business. Once again I heard nothing but the ticking of her bedside clock. Remembering that moment I still feel cold and sweaty.

'You should be able to hear a pansystolic murmur,' said the Professor encouragingly, 'telling you that Mrs Kennedy has an incompetent mitral valve.'

Once more I concentrated. I tried a little above the fifth intercostal space, and then just below it. Still I heard nothing. Then I moved to the right of the mid-clavicular line; to the left of it. Still I heard nothing.

'Can you hear it?' asked Professor Grainger.

I shook my head and continued to concentrate on Mrs Kennedy's chest. It was like a nightmare; a nightmare where safety always recedes as you get closer, where one horror follows another, where security seems totally unobtainable.

'You must be able to hear it,' insisted the Professor. 'She's still alive, isn't she?' There were polite titters from the collected nurses and students.

'I'll tell you in addition that Mrs Kennedy has some slight aortic incompetence,' he added.

'I think perhaps...' I began. 'Perhaps I can....'

'You can hear it?'

'Just...' I hedged again, reluctant to commit myself.

'The pansystolic murmur?'

'The pansystolic murmur,' I repeated.

'I'm afraid you can't, you know,' said Professor Grainger, with the smile of a cream-filled cat. 'Mrs Kennedy has dextrocardia. Her heart is not in the usual position; it's on the right-hand side of her chest, and you will find that her pansystolic murmur is to be heard there rather than in the more usual position on the left side of the chest.'

I stood open-mouthed and stared at him.

'Your first important lesson,' said Professor Grainger. 'If you're ever in doubt, always admit it; never allow anyone to persuade you that you can see, hear or feel anything that you can't see, hear or feel. And, if you're in doubt, ask for advice and help. A good doctor is one who's willing and able to admit that he's not omniscient, and who's ready to admit his own failings to himself and to others.'

I felt slightly cheated at the time — particularly when the Professor instructed the sister to remove his alarm clock and have it returned to his office; but afterwards, when the pain and indignity of the experience had faded a little, I felt grateful for the lesson. Nothing in medicine can be taken for granted and every doctor must always be on the look-out for the unexpected and the unusual.

That did not make the embarrassment and humiliation any easier to accept at the time, of course. As I shuffled shamefacedly back into the anonymity of the audience Professor Grainger led us on to the next patient. I learnt nothing else on Parkins Ward that morning, and so complete was my defeat that it was not until we moved to the male medical ward, a fifty-yard walk away from Sister Henderson's domain, that I began again to find myself listening to Professor Grainger.

'Mr Devlin is thirty-eight and, although he insists he is not fat, should be eleven feet tall to satisfy the insurance assessors who make up our weight-tables,' said Professor Grainger, allowing us the benefit of seeing one of his slyer smiles. 'Take a close look at him and see if you can tell me what he does for a living.'

We all stared like visitors at a zoo while poor Mr Devlin

pretended to read his newspaper.

'He has a good colour,' said someone. 'Is he a publican?'

'You mean he looks as though he drinks?' asked the Professor bluntly.

'His nose has a rather ruddy hue.'

'Do you drink, Mr Devlin?' asked Professor Grainger.

'I like a good whisky now and then.'

'Can we assume that all drinkers are publicans?' asked the Professor, directing his question generally.

'Most publicans are drinkers,' pointed out the student who'd made the original suggestion.

'Most medical students are male,' said the Professor. 'Does that mean that most males are medical students?'

'There are no callouses on his hands,' pointed out Hector. 'I doubt if his job involves any manual labour.'

'Good,' murmured the Professor.

Mr Devlin examined his right hand as though he'd never seen it before.

'Remove your pyjama jacket, if you please, Mr Devlin,' said the Professor.

'Is it anything to do with insurance?' asked a tall, straggly-haired student who always sported a bow-tie and whose name I could never remember.

'I'm sorry to disappoint you, Mr Young,' said Professor Grainger, who never forgot anyone's name, 'but this isn't Twenty Questions.'

'A wrestler,' suggested the only girl in our group, a delicate-looking creature who was more resilient and determined than she looked.

'Have you ever seen a wrestler?' asked the Professor.

Miss Charles admitted that she hadn't.

'Look at Mr Devlin's arms,' suggested Professor Grainger.

We looked at Mr Devlin's arms.

'Do you notice any difference between them?'

'He has a watch on his left wrist,' said Hector.

'And a ring on the little finger of his right hand,' I added.

'Look at the colour of his forearms,' suggested the Professor.

questions relating to his personal medical condition?"' the Professor interrupted him. He turned to the Minister. 'Medical students are often so very conscious of social problems,' he explained.

'Have you ever had a pain of a similar nature before?' asked Hector.

'There is certainly no doubt in my mind that the pain in my chest was unusually severe and disabling,' replied Mr Blake. 'It is naturally difficult to be precise about it since one's subjective assessments of the relative severity of any particular pains are incomparable. It is easier to compare or to contrast pains of a completely different nature.' Mr Blake paused. 'In particular,' he added thoughtfully, 'one has to recognise that as the memory of an incident of pain fades so may its importance.'

'Were you short of breath?' asked Hector, abandoning his previous question. He looked in desperation to Professor Grainger.

'In the House of Commons no one can afford to be short of breath!' smiled the Minister. 'And since there is said to be more hot air in the Chamber than in any airship ever built no Member can afford to allow himself the luxury of even admitting the possibility of such an occurrence.'

'You didn't find breathing difficult?'

'Ah!' said the Professor. 'Beware of the leading question! We must be careful not to put words in the mouths of our patients.' He reached forward and touched the Minister lightly on the arm. 'Particularly such eloquent and skilled speakers as Mr Blake.'

There was a silence then, the Professor and the Minister staring at Hector, clearly waiting for his next question.

'Were you sick?' asked Hector suddenly. It seemed a straightforward enough question. But Mr Blake was more than equal to it.

'Indeed I was,' he agreed. 'My presence on the ward can, I hope, be taken as adequate proof of my sickness.' He looked at the Professor. 'I'm pleased to say that I feel a good deal better today.' He clasped his hands across his ample stomach and smiled benignly at us all.

For a few minutes more Hector continued to attempt to question the Minister. The interrogation was finally brought to an end by Professor Grainger, who pointed out to us that Mr Blake had a considerable amount of paperwork to complete and that it was important that he rested.

'Now, remember,' the Professor said sternly, 'you're not to tire yourself or over-excite yourself. I'm allowing you to deal with your paperwork since I'm convinced that if we deny you access to your briefcase we'll be putting you under greater pressure than we are in allowing you a little more latitude than we might otherwise prefer.' He seemed to have picked up the politician's verbal habits.

'Don't you worry,' Mr Blake assured us all. 'These papers have a sedative effect.' He grinned to us and nodded. We edged away bemused. The rest of the round was something of an anticlimax, although an interview with an elderly gentleman who'd acquired penile frostbite during an extended performance of a singularly personal exhibition on an unusually cold autumn night made it possible for Professor Grainger to raise something of a blush on the cheeks of the petite Miss Charles.

After he'd left, hurrying away to give a brief press conference to reporters anxious for news about Mr Blake, Andrew and I stayed behind, waiting outside the sister's office for Dr Taylor to return. The registrar had left with the Professor, who hated to be seen in public alone; he would no more have appeared on a ward without his registrar than without his trousers.

'Did you notice something odd when he was telling us about Mr Devlin?' asked Andrew as we eyed a staff nurse with distinctive features and a pretty face arranging some flowers.

I was taken aback but thought for a moment. 'Perhaps I did,' I said.

'Shall we ask him?'

It seemed a good idea and together we went back on to the ward. Alone, I felt strangely vulnerable. When walking down the centre of a hospital ward it is difficult to tell whether the visitor or the patients are under closer scrutiny.

On the whole I think it's the visitor, who will usually keep his eyes on his feet, the flowers or one of the nurses, who gets more embarrassed.

'Hello again, Mr Devlin,' said Andrew. 'I'm Clay and this is Edward Vernon. We're medical students.'

Mr Devlin grinned at us. 'I remember.'

'You're a driving instructor?'

Mr Devlin nodded.

'Do you mind us asking you something?' Mr Devlin shook his head.

'Do you use a left-hand-drive car?'

Mr Devlin's grin grew wider. He shook his head again.

'But as a driving instructor you presumably spend most of your time sitting in the passenger seat?'

'That's right.'

'So surely it should be your left arm that gets hung out of the car window and gets brown,' I pointed out.

'I never have the window open,' said Mr Devlin. 'The car's got air conditioning.'

'Then why is it that your right arm is browner than your left?'

'I've been off work most of the summer and I've spent a lot of time sitting in the garden. We've got a small cherry-tree, and where I sit I'm partly in the shade.'

'Tell us one last thing,' said Andrew. 'Had the Professor met you before today?'

The driving instructor shook his head. 'But I'd met Dr Taylor,' he said, 'and he asked me what I did for a living.'

We thanked Mr Devlin and went back to wait for the registrar outside the sister's office.

Chapter Four

'The product we're testing is called Angipax,' said Dr Taylor, having returned from the press conference and led us along a maze of corridors to a small office in the basement. 'It consists of a combination of two well-tried drugs which haven't been used together before. The manufacturers believe that Angipax will help prevent angina as well as relieving the symptoms of heart disease.'

'What are the drugs?' asked Andrew.

'Erythrytyl tetranitrate and pentaerythritol tetranitrate,' said Dr Taylor without a stumble. 'The drug we normally use for angina sufferers is called glyceryl trinitrate. There seems a real chance that the specific combination that the manufacturers have developed will prove to have fewer side-effects and to be more effective as a prophylactic.'

'What do you want us to do?' I asked him.

'I'm doing a series of tests on about a dozen patients,' said Dr Taylor. 'Mr Devlin is the ninth in the series. I shall get him to work on this small treadmill without taking any Angipax and then do the same thing after he's taken the dose the manufacturers recommend.'

'And you just see when he gets his pain?' asked Andrew. He was standing on the treadmill which consisted of a continuous rubber belt on rollers designed to rotate at speeds of up to eight miles an hour. Anyone standing on the belt while it revolved would be effectively walking forward while actually staying just where he was. The belt was fitted with meters which enabled an observer to see how far the patient had walked and at what speed.

'That's more or less it,' agreed Dr Taylor. 'In fact it's a little more complicated than that. We're going to put a catheter into his heart before we begin the tests so that we can get a record of changes in pressure inside his ventricles.'

'Isn't that painful?' asked Andrew.

'Not at all,' the registrar assured us.

'You've got another patient for the trial now,' I pointed out.

Dr Taylor looked puzzled.

'Mr Blake,' I explained. 'He's had some heart trouble, hasn't he?'

'I think the Professor's keeping an open mind about Mr Blake's condition,' said Dr Taylor.

'Would you put him into the trial if you were certain that he'd had a minor heart attack?' asked Andrew.

'With his permission,' said Dr Taylor. 'We always make sure that the patient gives us permission before we start any trial.' He opened a drawer in a heavy wooden cabinet and took out a small cardboard box full of plain white pills.

'We'll test Mr Devlin for two days without the drug,' he said, 'and then we'll give him one of these every four hours. If the trial's successful, he'll be able to cope much more effectively with exercise and he'll be one of the first people to benefit from the drug.' The registrar put the box back into the cupboard. 'I've had a word with Sister,' he went on, 'and I want you to bring Mr Devlin down here tomorrow morning and tomorrow afternoon. Get him to exercise until he complains of pain. Measure the distance he's travelled and keep a note of it. Do the same thing the day after tomorrow and then for the two days while he's taking the drug.'

Dr Taylor then left the two of us alone to practise with the treadmill. Neither of us developed any chest pains but we both found ourselves breathless and sweating after a few minutes with the conveyor belt revolving at top speed. We were both, however, pleased with our good fortune in being selected to help assess such an important new pharmaceutical product.

Medical research projects invariably attract an enthusiastic response from all sections of society; doctors and patients share a belief that any research project must be worthwhile. The advances made by research workers over the centuries have been often dramatic and sometimes sensational. Everyone knows the story of Alexander Fleming hunched over his petri dish watching penicillin appear; similarly the exploits of Madame Curie and Monsieur Pasteur are known to us all.

In the past many medical researchers have experimented on themselves, using their own bodies as testing-grounds for their theories. A German called Pettenkofer swallowed millions of cholera bacilli in 1892 in an attempt to discover just how cholera attacked the human body. In the late eighteenth century a British doctor called White deliberately infected himself with bubonic plague, taking some discharge from a patient's suppurating gland, rubbing it into his own thigh and also putting some into a freshly and purposely made cut in his forearm. Pettenkofer lived but White died.

In 1797 an American, Dr Nathan Potter of Baltimore, soaked a cloth in the sweat of a patient dying of yellow fever and wore it wound round his own head for a whole night. When this failed, he scratched his skin and rubbed the sweat in. When that, too, failed he inoculated himself with pus taken from an abscess of another patient. He showed that yellow fever is not transmitted in any of these ways, but he certainly did not know that when he started his terrifying experiment.

Later a Dr Lazear allowed himself to be bitten by a mosquito which had dined off yellow-fever patients. He was less fortunate, for his theory was more accurate. He developed yellow fever and died.

In 1767 the great English surgeon John Hunter took some of the discharge from an infected male patient and gave himself venereal disease. In 1851 a young German doctor put matter from a patient with secondary syphilis into a superficial wound on his arm and died in great distress. In 1950 a Polish woman doctor, Clara Fonti, working in Italy, opened her blouse and rubbed one of her own breasts against the breast of a woman with fungating breast cancer. Dr Fonti did not die but she developed a serious case of blood poisoning.

But of course, all these experiments concerned infectious diseases, and it is less easy to deliberately give yourself a heart condition. Today's researchers can argue convincingly that they simply have to have patients for their experiments. And the patients are often willing, or at least rather reluctant to confess that they're unwilling. The patient who denies his doctors the chance to further medical knowledge will inevitably fear that he may have alienated the very people upon whom his life depends; while the patient who participates in a research programme is giving himself the chance to benefit from a major new breakthrough while at the same time passively making to human knowledge a contribution which he could never make actively.

Andrew Clay and I were convinced that Dr Taylor had given us our first opportunity to make a real practical contribution to medical knowledge.

Chapter Five

As the days of that first week went by, a rough pattern developed. Each morning at nine we'd wait for Professor Grainger and Dr Taylor outside the women's medical ward. At around twelve we'd finish the round on the men's medical ward. In the afternoons there were lectures to attend and, for Andrew and me, the experiments with Mr Devlin to conduct. Most important of all, there were patients to be clerked.

Each of us was given one female and one male patient to look after. This was inevitably far more for our benefit than for theirs and had little or no bearing on the management of any individual case. We quickly learnt that to conduct an examination effectively some system must be followed; asking questions indiscriminately is likely to be both time-consuming and unproductive, and a clinical examination which follows no pattern will, like disorganised prospecting, lead to the duplication of investigation in some areas and its total absence in others. Once a student had been given the task of taking a history from a patient and conducting an examination, he'd be expected to be able to provide the Professor's ward-round with up-to-date information about his or her progress. The Professor or, in the Professor's occasional absence, Dr Taylor would invite the appropriate student to explain and interpret the appearance of new symptoms or signs and to discuss with some understanding the various reports which came in daily from the pathology laboratory and radiology department.

The first patient I was told to study was Mrs Kennedy; I found her sympathetic and reassuring. I may have had little experience of patients, but she had had plenty of experience of medical students! For fifty years she'd been appearing annually in the finals examination-halls of several medical schools, her dextrocardia confusing and bemusing generation after generation of fledgling physicians.

Her congenital abnormality had affected her life in several different ways. Referred to a local consultant physician by an alert but puzzled family doctor when she was ten-years-old, she had been inside more than thirty hospitals in her life, despite the fact that she had only rarely been ill.

Her heart itself had never caused her any problem at all.

Even her marriage had come as a result of her abnormality. When nineteen-years-old and visiting a major London teaching hospital for an anatomy demonstration she had met young Harry Kennedy, a porter, who'd been instantly captivated by her beauty and charm. They'd married fifteen months later and moved into a small terraced house owned by the hospital.

Their only son had sadly been killed in France in the Second World War but, for years after that, they'd regarded a succession of medical students as their own. Then, four years before his retirement, Mr Kennedy had suffered a slight stroke. He'd made a good recovery from it but had been left with a limp and a slight speech impediment. Five years after his retirement he had another stroke, this one leaving him with a faulty memory and a tendency to forget where he was going if he set off from home alone.

Mrs Kennedy looked after him with an affection which came through clearly when she talked to me about him. She subsidised his small pension and their old-age pensions with the fees she received for appearing at medical schools and hospitals all over the south of England. She was too well-known to appear in higher-level examinations, but many students like myself had found her a puzzle.

It was not, however, her abnormal anatomy that had brought her into St Peter's, but the sudden appearance of a lump underneath her left arm. One advantage of appearing annually before a series of enthusiastic and careful student clinicians is that you receive an annual check-up at no charge. One of the students who had met Mrs Kennedy in the summer examinations had discovered her lump and reported it to the supervising Professor. The examiner had, in some surprise, checked and confirmed the student's findings. As a result Mrs Kennedy had been brought into the ward for a series of tests.

It was not until Thursday that the Professor stopped again

beside her bed.

'We've had the pathology report back,' I was able to tell him. 'It's quite benign.' I went on to explain that Mrs Kennedy's lump consisted of nothing more threatening than lymphatic tissue which had expanded under the influence of a simple infection.

'What else might we have expected to find?' Professor Grainger asked of no one in particular.

'Cancer?' suggested Hector.

'Go on,' nodded Professor Grainger.

'With a primary cancer site hidden somewhere, enlarged lymph nodes would be a sign that the cancer was spreading,' explained Hector. 'Or the lymph glands themselves might have turned malignant.'

'And what would the prognosis be?' asked the Professor.

'Poor,' said Hector. 'The patient is elderly and frail.'

The discussion of the theoretical possibilities associated with Mrs Kennedy's lump came to an abrupt halt with the arrival by Dr Taylor's side of a red-faced student nurse who whispered breathlessly in the registrar's ear. Dr Taylor nodded sharply, turned and whispered to Professor Grainger.

Instantly the Professor turned on his heel and began to head briskly towards the ward entrance. Dr Taylor followed him and the rest of us, after pausing uncertainly for a moment, scurried along behind him, like children following the Pied Piper. I hung back for an extra moment to squeeze Mrs Kennedy's hand and then hurried on with the others.

The Professor headed straight for the men's ward, where the only possible cause of such consternation could be the Permanent Under-Secretary, Mr Nicholas Blake. When we arrived, the house physician, Dr Tarrant, was standing anxiously by his bedside. Since she had direct practical responsibility for the male and female patients under Professor Grainger's care, Dr Tarrant wasn't expected to attend all ward-rounds, although she was expected to be readily available at little more than a moment's notice.

Mr Blake, it appeared, had begun to complain of a pain in his left calf while Dr Tarrant was on the ward taking blood samples. The nurse who'd answered his summons had immediately called the house physician, and she had immediately sent a message for the Professor. The Professor, of course, had arrived complete with a full set of students and paramedical specialists.

'It's rather swollen, sir,' said Dr Tarrant apologetically. 'And a bit red.'

'H'm,' the Professor sniffed.

'What is it?' demanded Mr Blake, white-faced and fearful. Beads of sweat stood out on his forehead. He was squeezing and pulling at a paper tissue.

'Does that hurt?' asked the Professor, gently pressing the Minister's left calf between his thumb and forefinger.

'It's very tender,' complained Mr Blake.

'H'm,' said the Professor again, pushing his thumb into the flesh just above Mr Blake's left ankle. It left a mark when he removed it; slowly the thumbprint filled up again.

'Tape,' snapped Professor Grainger, holding out a hand.

Dr Tarrant reached into the pocket of her white coat and produced an ordinary dressmaker's tape-measure. The Professor measured a point a few centimetres below Mr Blake's left knee-cap, marked it with a gold ballpoint pen he took from his waistcoat pocket and then measured the circumference of the Minister's calf at that point. Then he did exactly the same thing on the right calf.

'There's a two-centimere difference,' he said to Dr Taylor over his shoulder. Dr Taylor, who was carrying the Minister's medical notes, jotted down the information. Mr Blake had pulled the paper tissue into two parts; the sweat was hanging from his chin. The Professor slowly and deliberately rolled up the tape-measure, then handed it back to Dr Tarrant. 'You've developed a small clot there,' he said to Mr Blake.

'Is that dangerous?' demanded the Minister.

'It's something we must take seriously,' Professor Grainger said tactfully.

'I don't want any bull,' said Mr Blake scowling. He stared at the crowd of students around him. 'Do I have to put up with all these idiots?'

'My students?' asked Professor Grainger incredulously.

'Do you mean my students?'

With the paper tissue breaking up into lots of little pieces the Minister explained that he did indeed mean the students. Rather coldly and with more than a hint of a sniff Professor Grainger instructed us to leave. Obediently, albeit reluctantly, we backed away and headed with some embarrassment towards the ward entrance.

'Shall we take Mr Devlin down for his exercise?' asked Andrew as we passed his bed.

'It's a bit early,' I pointed out, looking at my watch. The readings were supposed to be taken at the same time each day.

'It's only an hour or so,' Andrew pointed out. 'It won't make any difference.'

We fetched a wheelchair from the corridor and helped Mr Devlin into it. Ten minutes later we were helping him on to the treadmill. The idea of taking him down to the basement in the wheelchair was to ensure that he arrived for each day's exercise rested and quite pain-free.

When we arrived back on the ward with him forty minutes later, the screens had been drawn around Mr Blake's bed and there was no sight of the Minister, the Professor or Dr Taylor.

I went back to the women's ward to see Mrs Kennedy again. Since the laboratory result had been negative I expected to find that she'd be going home before too long. To my surprise I found that she'd left already.

'We need the bed,' explained Sister Henderson. I felt rather sad that I'd missed Mrs Kennedy's departure but delighted that she'd gone home fit and well.

Chapter Six

My confidence was growing. No longer did the sight of a nightdress or a pair of pyjamas fill me with fear. I was beginning to learn my way around the hospital, and twice when visitors had asked me for directions I'd been able to help them. Like all major hospitals St Peter's had the facilities of a small village. There was a restaurant for the staff and another for visitors, a shop selling paperbacks, chocolate and ladies' hosiery, a bank for nurses and doctors on night duty and unable to get out to use ordinary banking facilities, a post office with a box reputed to be emptied only when it had been filled to the brim, a small church kept locked except on special occasions, a 'police department' manned by a series of sour-faced, blue-uniformed guards, and a recreation room for nurses which contained a table-tennis table and a record-player which didn't work. I was part of all this; a small part, it is true, but nevertheless a part.

There was, however, still one *bête noire* to be tamed. I hadn't forgotten my first night in the casualty department and I knew that somehow I had to exorcise that particular unhappy memory. Andrew had joined the editorial staff of the university newspaper and had left the flat to attend a meeting with his new colleagues, Hector had persuaded a student nurse from the female medical ward to accompany him to the cinema, and the flat seemed unbearably quiet without them. It was just a few days after my uncomfortable baptism. On the spur of the moment I decided to go to casualty once more.

Dr Crisp was on duty again. He smiled at me across a small crowd of arguing women and shrugged his shoulders.

'Weren't you here the other night?' he called.

I nodded.

'There was a club football match this afternoon,' he explained when I'd edged my way round the women. 'We've put the players back together, but now we've got half a dozen wives. One of them gave another a black eye and they started a free for all.' He thrust his hands deep inside his coat pockets and moved slowly away from them.

'There are a couple of porters coming along to move them out,' he said. 'I'm not getting mixed up in it.'

He introduced me to the casualty sister, a younger, prettier girl than the one who had been in charge on my previous visit, and poured me a cup of thick brown tea from a battered vacuum flask. I'd taken no more than two sips when the casualty reception-desk clerk came into the office. She had, she said, two new patients. A boy with a suspected fractured arm and a man who'd been cut by flying glass.

'I'll take the boy,' said Dr Crisp. 'You have a look at the bloke with the cut.'

Outside the office there was a considerable amount of noise. The porters had arrived and were trying to propel the shouting women towards the exit doors. They weren't having a great deal of success. My first casualty was sitting waiting in one of the half-dozen small cubicles set out along one side of the department. I looked at my watch as I entered the cubicle: it was eight o'clock.

'Hello, Doc,' said the patient, a thin dark-haired man with an old regimental tie on and an elderly Harris Tweed sports coat over his arm.

I started to tell him that I wasn't a doctor, but he wouldn't listen. I noticed in amazement that his eyes seemed to have independent suspension. They moved quite separately and it was impossible to decide which to look at.

I found it most disconcerting.

'Had a busy day, have you, Doc?' he asked.

I agreed that it had been fairly full.

'I've got the greatest admiration for you people,' he said firmly. 'I never let anyone get away with abusing the medical profession.' He looked straight at me so that I had to choose between the two eyes.

I murmured something about appreciating his support.

'Of course, I've had some illness in my time,' he went on. 'In 1956 I was in this hospital under Dr Jones. D'you remember Dr Jones?'

I shook my head.

'Real gentleman, he was. Real gentleman. I was in here for six weeks then. Varicose vein on the ulcer of the heart, it was, but they saved my life. When I left I told him, I said, “Dr Jones, I’ll have the greatest respect for members of your profession after this.” Very kind to me, he was. And a real gentleman as well. Always polite and courteous and never too busy to say “hello” or exchange a word or two with you.’

This made it difficult to try to persuade him to get to the point of his visit. In retrospect I rather suspect that I wasn’t the first doctor to succumb to this ploy.

‘There aren’t always people around who have sympathy for the genuinely ill,’ explained my patient. ‘I was in the Navy during the war and you didn’t get much sympathy there. The doctors weren’t too hot there, I can tell you. Of course they were officers and they didn’t take too kindly to dealing with us enlisted men. We used to look after ourselves most of the time.’ He smiled at me and raised his voice a little to make himself heard over the noise of the women arguing with the porters. ‘When we had lice we used to rub rum and sand into our hair.’

‘Right.’ I nodded, trying to get back into the conversation.

‘The lice got drunk and stoned themselves to death,’ he explained.

‘Ah.’ I’d noticed that one of his eyes was twinkling a fraction while the other was dull and motionless. I realized that the immovable eye was made of glass. ‘What’s brought you into casualty today?’ I asked, abandoning any idea of getting the question into the conversation tactfully.

‘You’re not going to believe it,’ said the patient with a sad shake of his head.

‘Try me.’

‘I’ve always been a careful driver,’ he told me. ‘There’s too much carnage on the roads. A lot of people seem to be happy to drive around drunk these days. I’m not one of those.’

I remembered that he was supposed to have a cut and I wondered where it was. He looked quite well, apart from the glass eye.

‘But it isn’t always up to the innocent, is it? You can

drive as carefully as you like and still get injured, can't you?'

I nodded.

'I'd been to the pub in Knibsborough village. D'you know it?'

I shook my head.

'Not to drink, you understand. Just to play a game of snooker. Just for a quiet evening with a few friends.' He carefully took the jacket off his arm and laid it down on the examination couch. His shirt sleeves were rolled right down to the wrist. 'On the way home I came through Little Tissington. D'you know it?'

I shook my head again.

'Beautiful village. Absolutely beautiful village with a delightful pond and a wonderful little Norman church. I was in a bit of a hurry because I wanted to get home to the wife. She understands me too well, you know, and gets a bit upset when I'm late for dinner. She always knows where I've been but always claims I've been with a woman. Now, do I look like the sort of fellow to do a thing like that?'

I had to admit that he didn't.

'Anyway, to cut a long story short, I was driving through Little Tissington when some damned fool farmer was moving his cattle around. Not your ordinary mild mannered milking-cattle but great bullocks. Bullocks! I ask you. At that time of night. On a public road.' He sniffed.

Outside the noise had subsided a little. It sounded as if the porters had done their job.

'I stopped,' he went on, 'but the bullocks didn't. One of them just threw himself straight at me. Right at the front of the car. Only had it for two years. Lovely little car, and the wife loved the colour. Well, they don't make cars to put up with that sort of weight, do they? The front of it just crumpled straight away. I'd got a bottle of whisky in my jacket pocket. Just for the wife really. Smashed, it was, smashed into little pieces. And the glass ruined my trousers. Mind you, if the glass hadn't done the job the whisky would have done. It smelt like a brewery in there. Of course, when the police came they could smell the whisky and they swore

I'd been drinking. There I was sitting in the middle of my ruined car, with my dinner spoiling and a broken bottle of whisky, and the police made me blow into one of their damned silly breathalyser bags. Impertinence, isn't it? Used to be that you were innocent until proved guilty. These days you're guilty until they prove you innocent. And they don't do that, do they? Well, the fumes of the whisky must have affected me. They only had to get the bag into the car and the crystals turned green.'

I looked at my watch. The time was nearly twenty minutes past eight. 'So you've got a cut on your leg?' I asked.

He was leaning forward to tell me more about his accident when the casualty sister poked her head round the cubicle curtain. 'Sorry to bother you, Doctor,' she said with kindly exaggeration, 'but there are a couple of people in the next cubicle who've just been brought in. Dr Crisp's busy in X-ray, and I wondered if you'd be kind enough to have a look at them for me?'

Honoured, flattered and pleased to get away from my story-telling friend for a few moments, I followed her into the next cubicle where a man who looked to be in his fifties and a woman of the same age were standing rather sheepishly by the side of the examination couch.

'Onions,' said the man, holding out his hand. 'Terence Onions.'

'Edward Vernon,' I said, taking it.

'This is my wife Christine,' he said, introducing me to his feminine companion.

'What can I do for you?' I asked.

'It's a rather embarrassing story,' began Mr Onions. I noticed that he was standing bent forward but assumed that it was simply a postural habit. He was, after all, rather taller than the average man. 'It's our twenty-fifth wedding anniversary,' he continued, 'and I was taking my wife out to dinner tonight to celebrate.' He swallowed and coughed.

'One of our friends runs a small bookshop and has a rather unusual sense of humour.' He was blushing now. 'He gave us a copy of a book of exercises,' he concluded with a rush.

'Ah,' I said, with some understanding.

'Well, when we were getting ready to go out we thought we'd perhaps try to, er, emulate the couple in the book. Try something new.'

'Right,' I encouraged him. 'Very sensible.'

'This is very difficult.'

'Don't be embarrassed,' I said. 'I'm used to this sort of thing.' I was having great difficulty in restraining the blush which I felt spreading across my cheeks. Naturally, since a blush is uncontrollable, I was doomed to fail in the end, but I felt that if I kept my cheek muscles under pressure I might be able to stem the flow of blood to some extent.

'My wife was in her underwear in the bathroom and I was reading the book waiting for her,' he explained. 'Perhaps we should have tried some of the simpler exercises first but we thought we'd try something we'd never tried before.'

'What happened?' I asked.

'It's my elbow,' said Mrs Onions.

'And my back,' added Mr Onions.

It turned out that, while struggling to complete a particularly imaginative exercise together, they'd fallen. Mrs Onions had cracked her elbow on the wash-basin and Mr Onions had fallen across the bath. I filled in forms, which I found on the small desk in the cubicle, requesting X-rays on the injured parts and told the couple to wait for a few moments. Then I left them alone and handed the forms to the casualty sister. I couldn't help noticing that Mrs Onions was wearing two-way stretch-elastic surgical stockings and contemplating the possible consequences had she been wearing something with more of an erotic flavour.

Back in the cubicle next door my story-teller was waiting for me.

'Of course, there was a silver lining in a way,' he went on. 'The whisky had sterilised the cut and it didn't get infected.'

'When did this happen?' I asked, rather confused.

'Six months ago,' he replied without hesitation.

‘Six months!’

‘That’s right. I had to have a tetanus injection at the time and then a second one six weeks after that. They said I should come back for a third injection six months after the accident.’

‘So you’ve just come for a tetanus injection?’

He smiled at me and nodded. I turned away and headed across the casualty department to the sister, whom I could see supervising the bandaging of an injured ankle. I explained to her that my patient needed a tetanus injection. Pausing for a moment, she plucked a small vial from a metal trolley and handed it to me. Then she took a syringe, a needle and a small pre-packed medicated swab from the lower shelf of the trolley and gave me those.

I swallowed air for a few seconds and then looked at the handful of simple equipment I’d been given.

‘What do I do with this?’ I asked, petrified.

‘Give him half a c.c. in his arm or his bum,’ she told me. She must have seen the look on my face, for she abandoned her bandaging again for a moment and put a hand on my arm. ‘Just take your time,’ she said, ‘and call if you’re in trouble. But really there’s nothing to it.’ This was the woman who’d called me ‘doctor’ a few moments before. I nodded my thanks and went back to give my first injection.

It wasn’t as bad as I’d feared. Neither the patient nor I fainted. He rolled up his sleeve as soon as he saw me enter. I wiped everything in sight with the medicated swab and transferred the right amount of fluid from the small glass vial to his subcutaneous tissue.

I had treated my first patient. Another major landmark in my medical education.

Chapter Seven

They'd been found sooner than she'd expected, when a neighbour had called round to see if they needed any groceries. The neighbour, quick-thinking, had flung the windows wide open and turned off the gas. Mrs Kennedy and her husband had immediately been rushed over to St Peter's by ambulance.

Neither of them had been poisoned fatally, but while partly conscious Mrs Kennedy had fallen and cracked a rib. The rib had pierced a lung and my very first patient was desperately ill. She was surrounded by several thousand pounds' worth of equipment, and a nurse had been allotted to sit with her.

Her husband was on the male medical ward where he occupied the bed in which the Permanent Under-Secretary had lain. When Professor Grainger had confirmed the diagnosis he'd made on the ward-round, that Mr Blake had a clot in a vein in his left leg, he'd begun treatment which necessitated putting up a drip. This had convinced the unhappy politician that he was doomed, and he'd abandoned his calm professional façade. He'd readily agreed when the Professor, who hated having his ward routine ruined by a patient who objected to medical students and insisted on having the screens kept drawn about his bed, suggested that he move to a one-bedded ward in another part of the hospital. No one told Mr Blake that the room was normally occupied by private fee-paying patients. Mr Blake and his political party were dedicated to the principle of socialized medicine for all and the abolition of fee-paying beds.

So there was a bed available for Mr Kennedy. The old man had suffered very little from the poisoning, but without his wife to care for him he was unable to stay in their home. When his wife had been in hospital before, he'd stayed with relatives. They were neither willing nor able to cope with him this time.

Mrs Kennedy was back on Parkins Ward and lying in the very same bed. This time, however, she had no smile for me or anyone else. She was unconscious and seriously ill.

Although we didn't know at the time what had happened, we managed to piece the story together later. Mrs Kennedy had always listened carefully to the doctors and students who had examined her. She knew more about some aspects of medicine than many of those charged with her care, but there were inevitably gaps in her knowledge. And as the object of discussions usually relating to the cardiovascular system and to congenital diseases Mrs Kennedy knew little about cancer and tumours in general. While she'd been lying listening to our discussion about her lump, she'd become convinced that the lump was cancerous. When we remembered the conversation we'd had around her bedside, we all agreed that, if we hadn't been called away to see the politician on the men's ward, the Professor would have concluded our session by reassuring her that the discussion had been purely academic and that her lump was quite harmless.

But Mrs Kennedy's fears hadn't been banished. She'd gone home certain that she was dying. And, in the silence and calm of her own home, her fears had grown. They were not for herself, but for her husband, who she knew would never be able to care for himself should she die first.

Rather than leave her Harry behind to be taken into a geriatric hospital or an old people's home, Mrs Kennedy had sealed the doors and windows of their tiny living-room with newspaper and sellotape, settled down with her husband to watch a favourite television programme and turned on the gas-fire without lighting it.

No one had told Mr Kennedy precisely what had happened. Dr Taylor had explained to him that he and his wife had been poisoned by a gas leak. A similar story had been told to the officer sent from the local police station. Professor Grainger, who'd once been fined for parking his elderly but stately Bentley in a no-parking zone while examining students at another medical school, disliked the police intensely. Since he'd also spent a good proportion of his life involved in litigation begun by a professor of pathology at an African medical school who'd taken objection to a book review written by Grainger himself, he also held a grudge against all lawyers. He was fond of pointing out that, if God had intended us to have lawyers, the Ten Commandments would have had amendments. He had no intention of allowing Mrs Kennedy to be taken to court on a charge of attempted murder.

And Mr Kennedy, whose memory was now so bad that he seemed to live entirely in the past, had been happy to accept this explanation.

For two days his wife hung on. She developed a chest infection which proved resistant to almost every antibiotic the hospital pathologist used in an attempt to control it. And slowly she grew weaker and weaker. She never regained consciousness and slowly she slipped farther and farther away from us.

The death of the motor-cyclist in the casualty department had affected me only slightly. I'd not known him alive and, in the harsh atmosphere of the casualty department, death had seemed almost inevitable. On the ward, however, I found Mrs Kennedy's death difficult to accept. It seemed somehow to be wrong for death to invade such a calm and organised place. Here were the best facilities available to mankind and presumably the best medical brains. Yet death was not to be denied.

I couldn't help blaming myself. It was I, after all, who'd been given the job of looking after her. It was I who'd introduced her to the ward-round on her last day in hospital. It was perhaps my fault that she'd left the hospital convinced that she was dying. A word from me and she'd have known better. She'd be sitting at home with her Harry.

It was not a responsibility I found easy to bear. It wasn't anything I'd ever been trained to deal with. But I'd learnt another important lesson: that patients will listen to their doctors and take the words they hear very seriously — whether or not they understand what they hear, and quite regardless of the fact that they may have misheard or misunderstood. The doctor, I'd learnt, has a tremendous responsibility to ensure that his patients understand him, for they will surely remember his words.

But the lesson, however valuable, did not make Mrs

Kennedy’s death any easier to bear.

Chapter Eight

Traditionally ward sisters are supposed to be stern, particular and rather humourless. Ordinary nurses, whether inexperienced students or fully qualified staff nurses with plenty of experience under their belts, are generally thought of as delightful companions and partners — always ready, willing and able.

Ward sisters, of course, have enormous responsibilities. It may be the doctors who decide upon the long-term care of patients, but it is the ward sister who looks after the patient's day-to-day needs. She it is who has the job of ensuring that his stomach remains full, his bowels empty and his bed tidy. She has the task of keeping two dozen patients immobile in bed and half a dozen nurses mobile and out of bed. She has to deal with irascible visitors and impertinent doctors and, since doctors, patients and visitors all share a permanent need for comfort and reassurance, she must be able to provide unending supplies of the milk of human kindness. To the people who enter her domain the ward sister must be all things maternal.

In a teaching hospital the unfortunate ward sister has the added task of coping with an unending stream of ignorant and often arrogant medical students. While she struggles with the unimaginably difficult task of managing her ward from day to day, she must also attempt to keep the students under some sort of control. So it is perhaps not surprising if she seems to be rather brusque, a little touchy about students leaving their litter in the middle of the ward, and unable to see the funny side of things when they change around all the patients' temperature charts.

And, of course, as a callow young student I was far less able to understand the ward sisters' problems than I am now, a comfortable time and distance away.

Apart from the sisters in the casualty department, I'd met just two ward sisters at this stage in my medical career. Sister Henderson, in charge of the women's medical ward, was about thirty-years-old, of slightly more than average height and with a backbone that a drill sergeant would have been proud to own. She had light-brown hair cropped short, serious brown eyes and rather tight, pouting lips. On her always immaculately smart dark-blue uniform she wore two small silver badges; her white starched cap was always pinned right at the front of her head. And, despite the camouflage provided by her uniform and the white starched pinafore she wore, it was perfectly clear that she had an absolutely enormous pair of breasts.

Sister Wills, who had the task of looking after the men's medical ward, was slightly taller, slightly darker and slightly slimmer than Sister Henderson. She also had a much less dramatic frontage.

In those early days and weeks I saw more of Sister Wills than of Sister Henderson, although I hasten to add that I never saw anything of either of them that was not secured underneath a uniform wrapping of blue calico. Andrew Clay and I had continued to take Mr Devlin down to the hospital basement twice a day for a week longer than Dr Taylor had originally intended. On two occasions the driving instructor had disappeared entirely from the ward for several hours while Dr Taylor had pushed thin tubes along his veins and into his heart. After those two experiments had been concluded, we'd had to abandon one or two sessions on the treadmill.

But it wasn't our visits to Mr Devlin which had given me the opportunity to spend more time on the men's ward as much as the admission of Mr Wills, the ward sister's father.

When he was brought into the hospital, Mr Wills looked ready for the mortuary rather than a hospital bed. It was so difficult to tell whether he was alive or dead that the nurse who accompanied him to his bed put out a cardiac-arrest call and, by the time he'd been helped off the porter's trolley and on to his bed, Dr Tarrant and Dr Taylor — together with another porter pushing a trolley loaded high with resuscitation equipment — were waiting for him. It was an impressive entrance. When it had been established that Mr Wills was indeed in the right department, I was allocated to watch his progress; Mr Devlin, one of my previous patients, had been discharged from the hospital and Mrs Kennedy had died. Only then did I discover the relationship between Mr Wills, until that moment a new patient who simply happened to have the unenviable privilege of being interviewed by me, and the ward sister.

Mr Wills was a chronic asthmatic, and the victim of two previous heart attacks. It was difficult to tell whether his pulmonary dysfunction was making his heart worse, or whether his failing heart was contributing to his pulmonary dysfunction. In addition, there was the problem of ensuring that the pills given to alleviate the symptoms of his heart condition did not exacerbate his lung trouble, and vice versa. Mr Wills was only in his mid-sixties but he looked twenty years older.

Dr Tarrant and Dr Taylor pushed one tube down his throat and another into one of his veins almost as soon as he arrived. They strapped an oxygen-mask across his mouth and injected stimulating drugs into a vein in the back of one of his hands. They also put a catheter into his bladder and had a nurse pin the collecting-bottle, an opaque plastic bag, to the bedclothes. After about an hour Mr Wills woke up, began to breathe a little more easily and started to look more like a patient and less like a cadaver.

Three hours after his admission he collapsed again. At the time his daughter was by his side, as was his wife, herself a former nursing sister. By the time Dr Tarrant and Dr Taylor had arrived with me at his bedside the two women had done most of their work for them. Sister Wills asked Dr Taylor if her mother could stay with her father and, when he agreed, added that she, too, would be staying on the ward with him, although she was due to go off duty that evening for forty-eight hours.

At nine o'clock the next morning they were both still there. Mr Wills was conscious, although only just, and his women looked almost as much in need of rest as he did.

During the night, said Sister Wills, he'd twice almost slipped away from them, and only Dr Tarrant's prompt arrival and the infusion of a diuretic had kept Cerberus at bay; the ungodly hound had certainly been snapping at his ankles.

At eleven that same morning he collapsed again, this time having a heart attack and disappearing from the land of the living with the stealth of a burglar. With much ado and many electrical aids he was dragged back again. Sister Wills had called the cardiac-arrest team and Mrs Wills had performed the closed cardiac massage until the arrival of the houseman and medical registrar.

By late afternoon Mr Wills' cheeks were hollow, his eyes dark and seemingly bottomless, and he looked, quite literally, like death warmed up. Dr Taylor and Dr Tarrant discussed him in the sister's office while the sister sat and held his hand. Dr Taylor pointed out that he'd suffered so much damage to his heart muscle that he'd never be able to leave the hospital and that there was more than a chance that he'd suffered some brain damage, too. Dr Tarrant reminded him that Mr Wills' daughter was the ward sister and asked him what he thought should be done. Dr Taylor sighed and agreed that there was nothing they could do but continue to respond to the demands and expectations of wife and daughter. I got the impression that if Mr Wills' daughter had been a librarian and his wife a shop assistant Mr Wills would have been left in peace.

That evening I sat with him while his wife and daughter ate in the staff restaurant. (The catering officer had in my brief experience sent round two memos complaining about staff members who described the restaurant as a 'canteen'.) For a moment Mr Wills opened his eyes, saw me standing alone and, with an effort that brought beads of sweat to his brow, shook his head from side to side. His eyes caught mine, and even in my innocence I felt they were the eyes of a man who knows there is no hope, knows that he must die and wants only to die quietly, quickly and painlessly. Guiltily I crept away.

Twice that night he died again and twice he was brought unceremoniously back to life. The electrocardiograph machine which stood on his bedside locker provided instant warning of impending doom, and at each interruption in this audible and visible record of his heartbeat, the alarm would sound and Mr Wills would be rescued once more.

The rest of the ward was almost forgotten. Professor Grainger spent nearly half his round talking quietly and confidentially to Mrs Wills and her daughter. They spoke alone in a distant corner of the ward while the rest of us stood around another patient's bed and half-heartedly discussed the various possible causes of an enlarged liver. Our hearts were not in it, of course; we were all too involved in the destiny of Mr Wills. All attention was on the curtain drawn around his bed and it seemed that all the hospital's equipment was stored in that small space. The other patients were unusually quiet and depressed. Mr Wills served as a permanent reminder of their potential fate and, each time he disappeared into a world beyond life, they waited nervously, as if they feared that they might disappear with him.

Mr Wills died during the eighth attempt to resuscitate him. He died at seven in the morning, with a tube down his throat, a tube in his urethra connecting his bladder to a plastic bag, a needle in each arm and one in his leg, a pair of defibrillating paddles by his side, a smear of grease on his chest, a scatter of broken vials and torn cellophane envelopes on his abdomen, an oxygen-mask on his face, an electrocardiograph machine on his bedside locker, a long cardiac needle in his heart, a smear of blood on his cheek and a puddle of spilt drip-fluid under his bed. He died lying on the floor with his arm in the puddle and his pyjama trousers around his ankles, his pyjama jacket ripped and his hair damp with sweat.

When I arrived on the ward, Sister Wills and her mother were still sitting in the corridor, consoling each other, while in the office the senior staff nurse sat trying to sort through the day's first problems.

'We did our best for him, Mother,' I heard Sister Wills whisper as she sipped a cup of tea. Although I didn't understand my doubts, I couldn't help wondering if the women were right.

Chapter Nine

Many times during those early weeks I found myself sinking into a deep dark depression. Until I'd begun my clinical apprenticeship I'd had little contact with death or illness. The first dead body I'd ever seen had been laid out on the dissecting-room slab and it had been all too easy to forget that the muscles, veins, arteries and nerves I dissected out had once belonged to a being filled with breath and ambition. Apart from the usual limited collection of infective childhood ailments, I'd been lucky enough to avoid personal experience of too much illness, and my relatives had little cause to take advantage of the youthful health service.

On the medical wards at St Peter's there had been, it seemed, nothing but a series of morbid encounters. Of the patients with whom I'd been closely associated only Mr Devlin had actually left the hospital and headed for home; the rest had gone to lie on the mortician's table. There had been too few opportunities for me to marvel at the wonders of medical science. Looking through the retrospectroscope, an instrument which enables the viewer to put past experiences into perspective, it's clear that a good many of the patients admitted to the medical wards in a teaching hospital will inevitably be seriously ill. Minor ailments, simple treatable infections, common or garden diseases, and illnesses requiring nothing more than rest, can be treated just as well, if not better, at home or in a local general hospital. The teaching hospital giants, specialists and superspecialists, aren't interested in simple pneumonias, uncomplicated stomach ulcers or strokes that are getting better. Theirs is a more complex world, where the treatment may be a success even if the patient dies.

It would have been easier, I suppose, had I come from a medical family. But no relatives of mine had ever practised medicine; the nearest we'd ever come were an uncle who'd made false teeth in his spare time, and a distant relative who'd driven an ambulance during someone else's war. I was still in short trousers when I first decided that I'd like to be a doctor. I don't really know why, although, when I attended St Peter's for my initial interview, I suppose I produced all the usual explanations: a desire to learn about the human body, a desire to help people, and so on. These are simplistic answers which do no justice to the truth. If anything, I suppose it was the relationships I saw binding my first family doctor to his patients which attracted me most. There seemed to me no better reason for living than to be a partner in so many complete and satisfying relationships. It was an interest in people as people, rather than as patients, which I first found attractive.

As those early clinical days went by I desperately wanted to discuss ethical, moral and philosophical problems with someone. I wanted to learn more about people, to understand the many and varied forces which drive doctors and patients and to obtain some insight into the relationships between those forces. But none of these subjects was in the syllabus. Nor was there likely to be any reward for original thinking. There were facts to be learned, techniques to be mastered and courses to be attended; the examinations which loomed ahead promised to be no more inspiring than crossword puzzles, the academic targets mere mental masturbation.

There was plenty of solid work to be done. There were patients to be interviewed and examined and books to be read; lectures to attend and ward-rounds to endure. After a day in the hospital there were textbooks to be taken out and notebooks to be scrutinised. My handwriting then was nearly as bad as it is now and many times I failed completely to read whole paragraphs I'd written.

But, more important than any of this, I needed to be at peace with myself; to understand just why I was studying medicine and to know that my early vocation was still intact. In the comfortable academic years of pre-clinical medicine it had been easy to be sure. There were no doubts then, just an overpowering eagerness to become involved in the clinical care of the sick and acquire the skills and knowledge which would give me the power to understand and help fight sickness and disease.

Now things weren't so clear. I wasn't so sure of myself, so certain that I wanted to be a doctor. My friends had fewer doubts. Hector was firmly set on his career, free and determined. He would qualify and take a house job in the teaching hospital before working abroad for a year. Then there would be a few clinical papers to write, a few lectures to give and a job as a registrar in St Peter's to obtain. Recognising his limitations, he'd decided to specialise in anaesthetics or radiology, the two specialities which offer the greatest chances for promotion and the most obvious opportunities for openings abroad. Neither an anaesthetist nor a radiologist needs to be able to speak to his patients. Both specialities can be practised successfully by a qualified man who's a confirmed monoglot.

Andrew had ambitions of a different kind. Brought up in a household where photographs of the most successful trade union leaders of the day took pride of place over the hearth, and where to be described as 'middle-class' was to be despised and derided, he claimed to be determined to be a genuinely socialist doctor, a physician with a social conscience. He had an overriding ambition to remain a member of the working class. Considering himself an agent behind enemy lines, he took great pains during the early weeks to ensure that his disguise remained convincing and absolute. Unfortunately he wasn't always successful in his attempts to disguise his true feelings. Once, for example, when Dr Taylor had half-jokingly suggested that a car worker with a persistent backache might have an active imagination and a disinclination to return to work, Andrew had defended the patient ferociously.

I envied them both their certainties and repeatedly despaired of my ability to cope with the ever-changing range of emotions I felt as I struggled to come to terms with the metamorphosis from student to doctor, from human being to physician. Sometimes I felt frustrated by the fact that in the last resort, medicine can only be an adjunct to the real purposes of living. The doctor merely puts people back on to the road of life; he stands by the wayside waiting for the frail and sickly to need his help. The greatest contributions in medicine add nothing to life and nothing to the healthy. Sometimes, too, I felt that it would be impossible to survive as a medical practitioner while still caring for the sick and dying. The death of Mrs Kennedy left me morose and inconsolable for days. And yet I also knew that I couldn't accept a life in which I didn't care, and didn't suffer with my patients.

They were tortuous, tortured days. I survived from day to day with my nose to the grindstone, my shoulder to the wheel, my ear to the ground, my head in my hands and my heart in my mouth.

Like all medical students, real as well as fictional, I survived by learning how to escape. Confused by death, mystified by life and uncertain about my role as an intermediary between the two, I became an enthusiastic party-goer. It provided no answers to the myriad of problems I struggled to solve but it did at least provide some respite.

There was, it seemed, always a party on somewhere. Either the nurses were celebrating the end of their examinations, the beginning of their examinations, someone's birthday or the first day of the month, or the doctors were celebrating the first day of Christmas, the last day of Lent, the retirement of some elderly honorary physician or the purchase of a barrel of beer. If neither the doctors nor the nurses were organising a party, then the medical students were; and, if there was no other available reason, the fact that at least one person wanted to have a party was considered a perfectly acceptable and valid one.

In the last week of our attachment to the medical wards, as we prepared to begin a series of visits to specialist hospitals, we had a leaving party in our flat; it was to be the first of several and as memorable as any.

The flat itself was situated on the ground floor of a large Victorian mansion more suitable for demolition than habitation. Owned by a rapacious landlord who had only a passing acquaintance with the public health by-laws, the building was divided into several separate flats. The others were all occupied by dental students.

Our flat contained three rooms, together with a bathroom whose plumbing would have felt at home in any nineteenth century country cottage, and a kitchen containing an ancient gas cooker covered with a half-inch layer of fat and a refrigerator which had no door and no cooling system but provided useful storage space for such daily essentials as cornflakes, baked beans, tinned beer and Stilton cheese. Hector, Andrew and I had a room each, deciding that the privacy this promised was preferable to the more usual sort of domestic arrangement involving separation into bedroom, sitting-room and dining-room. We ate in the kitchen and talked in each other's bedroom.

When invited to our party, Dr Taylor immediately offered considerable financial support, not on his own behalf but on behalf of the pharmaceutical company which had produced Angipax — the drug he'd been testing and which Andrew and I had helped him to assess. The company's only stipulation, that they be allowed to show a short film describing the virtues of one or two of their other products, seemed a small price to pay for two large casks of draught beer and a crate of red wine. The provision of two pounds of Cheddar cheese and a large French loaf Andrew, Hector and I assumed responsibility for; it seemed a modest outlay.

The pharmaceutical company representative, a portly fellow with a toothbrush moustache and a three-piece pinstriped suit, suggested that we begin with the film, preferring to show it to a small but relatively sober audience rather than to a large and inebriated one.

By eleven the representative, the beer and most of the wine had gone. Andrew had gone out to the local off-licence and bought half a dozen large cans of beer, and Professor Grainger, who'd made a brief visit, had brought with him a crate of stout. My problems and anxieties were beginning to succumb to the anaesthetic effect of an accumulation of alcohol. Such therapies may never be recommended by the medical profession, but they're often enjoyed by its members.

In the haze I found myself lying dreamily half underneath the kitchen table. The kitchen, like the other rooms, was full of people drifting freely about with the music. Most of the forms were indistinct, simply making up a writhing mass of human flesh. At some time during the night, however, a pneumatic blonde with enormous eyelashes and a charming lack of modesty lay down by my side underneath the table. She clutched an empty bottle of stout and snored incessantly.

Only in the morning, when I woke with cramped muscles and a hangover, did I discover that the lady with whom I'd innocently shared my patch of floor was Sister Henderson.

Chapter Ten

The next nine months were spent in four different hospitals: the Gregory Geriatric Hospital, the Hampton Grove Children's Hospital, the Women's Hospital and the Hilda Harper Hospital for the Mentally Ill. Hector and I remained together, beginning with the Geriatric Hospital. Andrew began at the women's hospital, and for weeks at a time I saw him only in passing as one or the other of us rushed into the flat to pick up books or clothes. Much of the time we were expected to live in the hospitals where we were studying, so the flat remained simply a centre from which we set off on our periodic peregrinations.

It was at the Gregory that I first slept in a hospital room. About ten feet long and five feet wide, it was equipped with a small, heavily stained dressing-table decorated with footprints left by a score of coffee cups and containing four drawers, lined with old newspapers, which resisted all attempts to open them more than a few inches; a wardrobe whose door swung open every time there was any slight movement elsewhere in the room; and a bed which creaked and squeaked as I breathed. The room was illuminated by a window which didn't shut properly and was edged by curtains which didn't meet, and by a sixty-watt bulb suspended shadeless from a fraying cord which hung from the centre of the ceiling. The walls, painted a hideous shade of yellow many years previously, had a mark halfway up beyond which the woman responsible for cleaning the room obviously could not reach, and in places the peeling paint had disappeared altogether, allowing pieces of the original wall-covering to show through. Underneath the yellow paint was brown paint. The floor was covered with thick linoleum, patterned in blue and green and cracked in several places. It was so dirty that I'd never have dared walk on it with only my socks to protect me.

The room had no washbasin, no chair and no table. There was, however, an old-fashioned black bakelite telephone standing on a ledge just inside the door. When it rang, the occupant of the bed had to climb out, find his shoes and pad across the floor to either the telephone or the light switch. Washing facilities were provided in a single room twenty yards down the corridor where a lavatory, a washbasin and a bath were shared by the students in residence, the resident doctors and assorted members of the nursing staff. The fact that all the toilet facilities were in the same room meant that in the morning there was a considerable demand for it; at eight o'clock a dozen or so heads could be seen peering round their half-open doors, watching for a sign of someone leaving the bathroom. When its door handle began to turn, a scrummage of doctors, nurses and medical students would appear in the corridor, dressed in various combinations of nightwear, underwear and uniform.

The walls of the bathroom were cleaner than those in the bedrooms since the condensation had long since removed all the paint, leaving behind bare areas of cracked plaster. There was only one plug, so that if you wanted to use the bath you had to take it from the washbasin, and vice versa. For some reason best known to the designers, when the washbasin was emptied water flowed up from its waste-pipe into the bath. All in all, the plumbing in the residential quarters of the Gregory Geriatric Hospital had much in common with that in the flat I shared with Andrew and Hector.

My responsibilities towards the patients in the hospital were fortunately limited; I was able to allow those with more urgent needs and more responsible tasks to slide into the bathroom before me. And the telephone didn't prove too much of a problem; during my stay in the room it rang only once, and that was a mistake.

The patients were, of course, all elderly and frail. Most of them had been admitted as a last resort, simply because they weren't ill enough to take up beds in ordinary general hospitals and not well enough to look after themselves or stay in a residential home. It was perhaps unfortunate that I'd been sent to a geriatric hospital after my maudlin introduction to clinical medicine. The urine-heavy atmosphere, the lack of equipment and nurses, the dreadfully dreary surroundings and the sense of despair which seemed to hang over the whole place did nothing to raise my spirits.

In self-defence my memory seems to have erased most of the experiences I had there, although one unusual event does linger.

It happened on an unusually warm winter day. Hector and I had discovered two croquet mallets and a set of hoops and balls in a small cupboard next to the hospital canteen. Desperate for excitement, we'd found a relatively flat piece of lawn, hammered in the hoops and begun to play a game which, I have to admit, bore relatively little resemblance to the one for which the equipment had been manufactured.

We'd just succeeded in hitting a ball each through one of the hoops when I saw one of the auxiliary nurses racing along the path towards us. She was waving and shouting, and puffing and panting for breath.

'There's been an accident...' she managed to mumble. 'Mr Tidy's cut himself.'

Throwing down the mallets Hector and I crowded round her.

'Who's Mr Tidy?' asked Hector.

'How bad is the cut?' I asked.

'Where is he?'

'How did he do it?'

'Have you found one of the doctors?'

'When was it?'

'I don't know,' cried the auxiliary nurse. 'Sister sent me to find a doctor.'

'We aren't doctors,' said Hector.

She began to cry.

'Where is he?' I asked. She told us that he was on one of the men's medical wards and, when we asked which, began to give us complex, incomprehensible directions. The Gregory Geriatric Hospital, like many others with similar functions, consisted of one enormous old Victorian building with numerous additions. It is extremely easy to get lost in one of these places despite the notices and instructions posted at strategic intervals along all the corridors. Eventually the nurse agreed to lead us back to the ward she'd left. As she half-walked and half-ran she explained breathlessly that Mr Tidy was one of the male charge nurses (the masculine equivalent of sisters) and that he'd cut himself while trying to pull a rubber incontinence pad out of the filing cabinet in which it was kept. He'd been cut on one of the shelves. Neither Hector nor I wanted to add to the confusion by asking why the rubber incontinence pad was kept in a filing cabinet.

When we arrived at the scene of Mr Tidy's embarrassment we discovered he'd disappeared.

'Sister's taken him to the main entrance,' explained a voluntary helper, putting library books into neat piles on a table in the centre of the ward. None of the patients had read a book for years but the rules stated that library books should be made available to them regularly.

Led again by the nurse, we set off for the main entrance.

As we ran we could see the occasional drop of blood on the corridor floor. Hector bent down once and checked to see whether it had clotted.

'They aren't far ahead,' he called as we raced on.

As we arrived, all quite breathless, at the main entrance, we were just in time to see an ambulance disappearing down the drive. The nurse was so exhausted that she slumped into a heap on the floor.

'Was that Mr Tidy?' asked Hector, rather red in the face as a ward sister walked slowly back in. She looked rather surprised and then nodded.

'Where's he gone?' asked Hector.

'I've sent him to the casualty department at St Peter's,' explained the sister with a sniff. 'We don't have a casualty department here and I think he'll need a stitch in his finger.'

'Just one?'

'Perhaps two,' she said defensively. 'What are you doing here, anyway? You're students, aren't you?' She managed to put a lot of feeling into the word 'students'.

'The nurse said you wanted a doctor,' said Hector. 'We thought we might be able to help.'

'You can,' said the sister. 'I just wanted someone strong to help me get the damned incontinence pad out of the filing-cabinet.'

After the Gregory I went to the women's hospital, where

I found life far more rewarding. It included a large maternity department and, since pregnancy isn't an illness and childbirth is a cause for celebration rather than mourning, there was less unhappiness there than I had grown to expect in any hospital. It was there that I performed my first full examination of a woman, losing my professional virginity to a kindly young mother of two who bore with remarkable patience my clumsy attempts to discover her cervix. Before I approached her bed I'd been warned by Hector, a normally humourless young man whose ambitions were entirely clinical and orthodox, to prepare myself adequately for the examination. He told me confidentially that I had been unfortunate enough to be allotted to a young woman of unusual dimensions, and warned me to roll my sleeves up as far as they would go and to be sure to wash up past my elbow before beginning the examination. He even offered to look after my watch for me.

As I approached Mrs Jessop's bed I headed straight for the washbasin, removing my white coat and hanging it carefully on a mobile screen which had been already arranged around her bed. She watched in some amazement as I carefully rolled up my shirt sleeves, and then stared at me with horror in her eyes as I proceeded to lather my arms well past my elbows.

'What are you doing?' she asked quietly.

I explained that I wanted to make sure that my hands were clean before I performed the examination.

'Aren't you going to put gloves on?' she asked.

'Yes,' I said, 'but they only reach up to my wrist.'

There was a pause of several seconds before Mrs Jessop let out a yelp. Hector sprained an ankle as he attempted to escape down the stairs at twice his normal speed. I got my revenge two days later by piling two tables, eight chairs, a fire-hose and two buckets full of water outside his room at midnight, then telephoning him to let him know there was an emergency involving one of his patients.

The remainder of this part of my life was consistently underwhelming and forgettable. After the women's hospital I went to the children's hospital. At a party at the children's hospital I met Sister Henderson again, this time accompanied by Dr Crisp, the casualty officer. She looked puzzled when I approached her, and asked me if we'd met before.

Chapter Eleven

It had been a fortnight since I'd seen Andrew. We met in the kitchen over a bowl full of pancake mixture and a bottle of cheap wine that he'd bought at a garden party organised by the Friends of St Peter's Hospital. The party was supposed to raise money for the staff to buy equipment and the administrators to buy luxuries such as chairs for the wards. If they sold many bottles of wine like the one Andrew had bought, they probably provided the hospital with more new patients than new equipment.

Andrew had just completed a tour of the same four hospitals as I'd visited, and his experiences contrasted with mine. He'd found the women's hospital depressing, the children's hospital invigorating, the geriatric hospital inspiring and the mental hospital enormously attractive. His experiences at the last, however, were undoubtedly influenced by a blossoming relationship with a twenty-year-old girl recovering from an attack of depression. Two days before her discharge, Andrew had arranged to meet her for dinner at a Chinese restaurant. Despite all the odds, their romance flourished.

The main topic of conversation, however, was not the developing relationship, but the Angipax research project which Andrew and I had assisted with. He was particularly disturbed by the fact that he'd discovered that Mr Devlin, the driving instructor whom we'd accompanied to the St Peter's treadmill, was being called back to the hospital for routine cardiac catheterisations.

Andrew and Mr Devlin had met accidentally in the corridor outside the staff dining-room. As a habitué of the hospital Mr Devlin preferred that to the visitors' restaurant, having discovered that its portions of chips were larger.

'He's been back at work for weeks,' said Andrew. 'He still gets attacks of angina, but since he works mainly sitting down he doesn't have too much exercise. As long as he avoids the more imaginative learner drivers he doesn't get too much trouble with pains.'

Dr Taylor, Andrew went on to explain, had persuaded Mr

Devlin to reattend the hospital once a month for tests. These included work on the treadmill and sessions which involved pushing special tubes along his veins into his heart. Mr Devlin, Andrew said, dreaded and hated these particular experiments. Once he'd had a cardiac arrest and, when he'd woken up, he'd found himself nursing three fractured ribs, produced by the enthusiastic thumping on his chest.

'It really isn't right,' insisted Andrew. 'I asked Dr Taylor why Mr Devlin had to keep having cardiac catheterisations and he told me they hadn't completed the trial. The poor chap's going through agony just so that Dr Taylor can finish writing his research paper, and he thinks it's all being done to help him.'

I pointed out that there wasn't much we could do about it, even if we wanted to.

'There's a hospital ethical committee,' said Andrew. 'I looked up the details in the library. They're supposed to keep an eye on all research done in the hospital and make sure it's all necessary and worthwhile. They're also supposed to make sure that all patients know exactly what's going on and that they don't suffer at all.'

'Who's on the committee?' I asked him.

'All sorts of people. Most of them I'd never heard of, but I know the chairman.'

'Who's that?'

'Professor Grainger,' he replied with a shrug. 'That's why I haven't bothered complaining to them. The Professor's hardly likely to take my side against his own registrar, is he?'

'There you are, then. What are you going to do?'

'I don't know,' he admitted. He poured two more glasses of dreadful wine and poured some more pancake mixture into the frying-pan. Hector, who had a magnificent talent for homing in on anything edible, arrived just as the pancake was being divided and sprayed with lemon juice. It was the first time the three of us had been together in the flat since we'd completed our initial period on the medical wards; the first time, in fact, since our celebratory party.

Hector said that the sight of pancakes reminded him of

the time he'd been on one of the wards at the geriatric hospital at lunch-time. As a special treat the chef, who'd been about to leave to take a job as an assembly worker at a car factory, had prepared individual pancakes for all the patients. Most of them, said Hector, had been strong enough to use as footballs if wrapped around lumps of hospital rice pudding, but that was beside the point.

The lunches, Hector went on, had been taken around the ward by the sister and her only assistant, a young student nurse who'd been working in the hospital for less than a week. The sister handed out pancakes on the left-hand side of the ward while the nurse dealt with the right. (Hector, presumably, had sat in the office with his nose turned up.) Three-quarters of the way through the distribution the junior nurse hurried up the ward and whispered to the ward sister that one of the patients she was serving had died before he'd even managed to start his pancake. She wanted to know what she should do. Coolly and calmly, the sister told her to give his pancake to the next patient and to keep the remaining one for herself.

Hector roared with laughter when he told this story, but Andrew didn't find it amusing at all. He said it had put him off his meal completely since he found it in such bad taste. As he tucked into Andrew's share, having sprinkled it with a liberal helping of sugar, I couldn't help thinking that Hector had told the story on purpose.

Andrew spent most of the time talking about Sara, the girl he'd met at the mental hospital, and arguing with Hector, who said it was unethical for him to develop a personal relationship with any patient, but particularly one recovering from a depressive illness. Andrew didn't mention Mr Devlin again, and I thought he'd forgotten the affair; but, just before we all went to bed, he said, 'I still feel bad about Mr Devlin. I wish there was something we could do about him.' I was tired and I didn't take much notice. Perhaps I should have done.

Chapter Twelve

The itch at the back of my neck was slowly driving me mad. My only consolation was that I could get rid of the itch on the sole of my left foot by rubbing it along a bar fixed on to the bottom of the operating-table.

For what seemed like a month I'd been standing beside Archer Meridew, the consultant surgeon at St Peter's, as he struggled to corner and remove the gall bladder from Mrs Potter, a forty-two-year-old around whose ample form Puck would have taken considerably longer than forty minutes to put a girdle. While Mr Meridew and his registrar Simon Grant fiddled and fussed with Mrs Potter's seemingly unending layers of fat, I was kept busy snipping lengths of thread and acting as a butt for the surgeon's cruel sense of humour. I'd cut the stay sutures designed to hold things in place, I'd dropped the slippery instruments given to me to hold, and all in all neither Mr Meridew nor I found the experience a pleasant one. I was beginning to understand one of the lesser-known advantages of wearing a surgical mask: the surgeon doesn't know the name of the assistant who's hampering him unless he actually asks.

My arrival in the operating-theatre at two minutes to nine had not been auspicious. As I scrubbed away at my hands I'd awaited Mr Meridew's coming with some trepidation. Having been a consultant surgeon at a major teaching hospital for twenty years, Archer Meridew had acquired a reputation for bluntness. As a student with absolutely no experience at all of operating-theatres, I wasn't looking forward to being shredded; I couldn't help thinking of another medical student who, so legend had it, had been so incensed by the surgeon's criticisms that he'd swung him a right hook in the middle of a vagotomy and pyloroplasty. Mr Meridew had been knocked out for twenty minutes, the registrar had had to finish the operation, and no one knew what had become of the student.

As I scrubbed slowly away a junior theatre nurse stood over me. It reminded me of my childhood, when I'd been getting myself ready for a children's party. She even wanted to check my fingernails. When, having finished to her satisfaction, I allowed the soapy suds to be rinsed off my forearms down past my hands, I heard her tut-tut behind me. She explained that they had to be allowed to drain off my elbows, not across my freshly cleaned hands. I had to go through the scrubbing procedure again; by the time I'd finished my hands were so sore and raw that I hardly knew what I was doing. But I turned the taps off with my hand rather than my elbow.

Getting dressed after my third attempt at washing proved equally tedious. The kindly but meticulous nurse put on the hat and mask I should have donned before I'd started scrubbing, adjusting the ties so that they fitted comfortably but firmly behind my head. Then she helped me into my gown.

Putting on skin-tight surgical gloves is something which a contortionist would demand extra money for; doing it without touching the outside of the gloves demands skills a pickpocket would be proud to possess. Take it from me that anyone dexterous enough to be able to dress in surgical garb is perfectly capable of dealing with your appendix or brain clot. The gloves come with small packages of chalk dust or talcum powder which you're supposed to sprinkle on your hands before attempting to don the gloves. I managed to spread a cloud of dust over myself and the nurse, and to put a little on my left thumb.

Eventually I managed it all; but not before I'd ripped three pairs of gloves into ribbons, poking my fingers through the thin rubber. Then I was ready for my first entrance.

I honestly still had no idea at that point that Mr Meridew was in the hospital, let alone in the operating theatre, and I waltzed merrily through the opaque plastic swing doors humming happily to myself. Mr Meridew, who was busily bent over an open abdomen searching for a small hole in someone's bowel, threw a dirty swab at me with astonishing speed. Automatically I reached out for it and, to my surprise, caught it. That meant that I now had to go back and get changed and washed again. By the time I'd reattired myself in sterile surgical green the operation was almost over. I entered the theatre as Mr Meridew put the last suture into the patient's skin and pulled off his gloves with a resounding snap. The theatre sister, a kindly woman with a tic which made every male think she was winking at him, let me sit in a corner waiting for the next patient to come in. It was the gargantuan Mrs Potter.

* * *

'What's this?' demanded Mr Meridew.

I was daydreaming and had no idea he'd spoken to me.

'What's this?' shouted Mr Meridew, whose patience was far from inexhaustible.

I peered into the mysterious dark depths where my hands were buried among a confusing variety of internal structures. I could just see the surgeon's index finger pointing down towards the base of the hole.

'It's the retractor,' I said.

'The what?' he spluttered.

'It isn't the retractor,' I whispered.

'What do you eat with onions?' he shouted.

'Peppermints?' I suggested, after thinking for a moment.

'Liver, you fool!' he roared.

It wasn't a good beginning to our relationship. Particularly since I'd just been allotted to Mr Meridew's surgical 'firm', or team, for the next few months. I and half a dozen other students would be expected to take it in turns to attend his outpatient clinics, assist him during operations and accompany him on his wards. We'd all be expected to talk to and examine his patients before and after their operations. For some reason, whereas a medical student working with a physician is known as a clerk, one on a surgical firm is known as a dresser. I suspected that these terms originated in the days when they performed real and useful functions during their years of apprenticeship. Today's medical student usually plays as important a part in a patient's survival in hospital as a student of Serbo-Croat.

Both Hector and Andrew were delegated to Mr Meridew's firm with me. On that first morning, as I stood alongside the great man himself, Hector was busy looking at the collection of miscellaneous lumps and bumps collected by Mr Meridew's house surgeon for his own surgical list the following day and Andrew was taking blood samples from the patients awaiting more major surgery.

'I'm sure this damned table is moving up and down,' bawled Mr Meridew, standing back from the patient for a moment. His registrar stepped back with the consultant and put his head on one side as he examined the table from a distance. He looked at it as if half-expecting it to blow up in his face.

'Come on, Archer,' called the anaesthetist, a huge bear of a man sitting at the head of the table and sharing his attention between the bank of dials and pieces of machinery and a book of crossword puzzles. Occasionally during the operation he'd ask out loud if anyone knew the answer to a clue that was puzzling him. Mr Meridew hadn't been able to help at all, but one of the theatre technicians had proved an adept aide. The anaesthetist, Jim Kibble-White, had masses of golden curly hair which hung out from his surgical cap on all sides. I'd heard a good deal about him since a niece of mine had once had an operation for which he'd anaesthetised her. He'd given her a piggy-back to the operating-theatre instead of making her ride on the trolley the porters had brought to the ward and, during the operation, he'd wrapped her teddy bear up in swathes of bandages so that when she came round she could nurse it better. He was slow and rather untidy but he had a tremendous reputation as an anaesthetist. Hector said he rather hoped that when he was assisting there would be a crisis so that he could see Kibble-White in action.

'It isn't you that's got to work on the damned table,' muttered Mr Meridew to him.

'The blood'll be out of date if you don't hurry up,' insisted the anaesthetist.

'It's all easy enough from where you are,' shouted Mr Meridew crossly. 'You try operating with a knife that isn't sharp enough to cut butter in a heatwave.' The long-running feud between the two was well known in the hospital.

Kibble-White enjoyed baiting the surgeon, who never seemed to realise what was going on and who always rose, like a hungry trout, to the slightest flick of the fly.

I watched with horror as I saw the registrar put his foot on a bar under the table. The table responded and moved up an inch or two, taking the patient that much farther away from the floor. Then the registrar moved the bar in the opposite direction. This time the table went down a little. I felt myself blushing underneath my mask. The bar was the one I'd been using to scratch my foot. It was no wonder the table had been going up and down like a yo-yo. Fortunately for me neither of the two surgeons was prepared to investigate any further. Having readjusted it to suit themselves they went back to work.

Three-quarters of an hour later it was all over; the gall bladder lay on a small tray by the patient's side and the appalling hole in Mrs Potter's abdomen had been closed. Mr Meridew had even let me put my forefinger on one of the knots he'd tied. Another landmark in my career. Then he and Mr Grant hurried off to look at a patient on the ward who was recovering from an operation the day before.

Helping the theatre sister to clear up, I picked the redundant gall bladder from the tray and threw it into a bucket containing dirty swabs and little pieces of excised tissue. The gall bladder had been cut open and inside it I could see half a dozen stones nestling comfortably. The theatre technician who'd proved such an adept crossword puzzler took the bucket away to the hospital incinerator.

Just five minutes after he'd disappeared, a young nurse from the surgical ward came up as I was standing by the anaesthetist's trolley and listening to Dr Kibble-White's explanations of the purposes of the various dials and gauges.

'Mr Meridew says could he please have the stones from Mrs Potter's gall bladder to give her when she wakes up.'

'They're round here somewhere,' said the anaesthetist, taking from the bottom of his trolley a small glass bottle which was clearly there for just that purpose. It even bore a label marked 'Mrs Potter'.

'They aren't,' I whispered, sweat beginning to run down my nose.

'Aren't they?'

‘I’ve thrown them away,’ I confessed, and told him what had happened.

‘Wait there a minute,’ he said to the nurse. He winked at me and hurried off. Two minutes later he came back with half a dozen small stones in the palm of his hand. He put them into the bottle and ceremoniously handed it to the nurse. She in turn hurried off, holding the bottle carefully, as if it contained some delicate and rare archaeological discovery.

‘You got there in time?’ I said. ‘Thank heavens.’

‘I didn’t even try.’

I looked at him, uncomprehending.

There’s a gravel path outside,’ he grinned.

Chapter Thirteen

For centuries physicians have rather looked down their noses at surgeons, regarding the branch of the profession which involves cutting people up as crude, barbarous and quite devoid of finesse. English physicians had their own Royal College in 1518, but surgeons had to wait until 1800 before they could boast of a college with sovereign patronage. Whereas the physician considered himself a man of some social standing, the surgeon had to be content with purely financial rewards, being seen as a craftsman rather than a professional man.

Partly as a reaction against this tradition of inferiority, many modern surgeons seem to exude a mixture of arrogance and self-confidence which makes Muhammad Ali look positively modest and withdrawn. Surgeons, I discovered, are the ones who dress flamboyantly, showing a penchant for coloured waistcoats, bow-ties and patterned shirts. Physicians, on the other hand, are more likely to stick to pinstriped suits, white shirts, club ties and perhaps the occasional carnation or rosebud. Outside the operating-theatre, Mr Meridew (and surgeons always drop the courtesy title of 'doctor' when they become fellows of the Royal College of Surgeons in memory of the fact that, a century or two ago, surgeons were not allowed to call themselves doctors or join the existing august colleges) dressed to fit the popular image of a successful surgeon. He wore a three-piece suit of either pale blue or beige and a pastel-coloured bow-tie contrasting with his shirt. He never wore a white coat, although he always insisted that his subordinates should do so, but often appeared on the ward or in his outpatient clinic wearing his green surgical garb. With rubber boots on his feet, a cap pushed to the back of his head, a mask around his neck, and with dark patches of sweat underneath his arms and in the small of his back, he always looked as though he'd just come from saving a life. Occasionally there'd be just a couple of drops of blood on the front of his theatre shirt.

Although he was slightly above average height anyway,

his ordinary shoes or boots always had heels specially built to give him an extra inch or so more. He took a dislike to me when we first met without masks, perhaps remembering my first appearance because of my height. Or it may have simply been that he automatically disliked anyone taller than himself.

Fortunately for me, he spent most of his time at his private consulting-rooms and at a private nursing home some two or three miles away which was equipped with its own operating-theatre suite. That meant that I found myself attending clinics and ward-rounds with the senior surgical registrar, Mr Grant, who, although he was preparing himself for life as a consultant surgeon, was still young enough and human enough to remember the trials and heartaches a medical student has to endure.

Simon Grant it was who allocated new patients to the students, so it was from him that I received instructions one Thursday morning to take a look at a schoolteacher in the third bed along on the left.

In my early months as a medical student, I'd already developed a technique of recognising a patient's occupation simply by looking at him carefully. Schoolteachers were among my favourite categories of employed persons since I was convinced that I could identify one at twenty paces. It wasn't the chalk dust, the collection of cheap ballpoint pens in the breast pocket and the invariably frayed cuffs that gave it away, so much as the air of mystified and confused innocence borne with a sense of omniscience. Schoolteachers spend their time with children, of course, and so develop a type of arrogance, mixed with weary patience, that is unique. When they're in the company of other adults their sense of superiority is damaged and they show some confusion.

As I wandered on to the surgical ward, ready to begin my examination of my new patient, I was looking for the telltale signs — all the more difficult to discern on a hospital ward where everyone dresses in pyjamas and wears a worried look. There was absolutely no doubt about it. The patient in the third bed along was a schoolteacher. Small, thinning on top, rather red-faced and wearing a pair of steel-rimmed spectacles, he was easily identifiable. There was no doubt about it. He'd taught me physics for three years.

'Mr Tucker!' I said, stopping still at the foot of his bed and staring along the sheets at the familiar face that had for several terms struggled to encourage me to show a little more interest in the mysteries of magnetism and reflected light.

'Vernon!' exclaimed my former teacher. 'Edward Vernon, isn't it?'

I nodded. I felt rather self-conscious in my white coat and the striped waistcoat I'd taken to wearing since I'd begun work on the surgical wards. I'd bought it in a sale at a small tailor's near the hospital and had never quite got used to it. I buttoned my white coat firmly around me and tugged at my tie.

'What are you doing here?'

I explained that I was a medical student.

'Medicine, eh?' nodded Mr Tucker with a slight smile. 'I thought you'd gone off to study veterinary medicine. I wonder why I thought that.' He scratched at his head. 'Must have got you confused with someone else.'

'Actually,' I began, rather embarrassed now, 'I'm supposed to examine you and ask you a few questions.'

Mr Tucker looked at me and frowned slightly. 'You're not my doctor, are you?'

I shook my head.

'I didn't think you'd left long enough,' he smiled with some relief.

'I'm just starting my clinical work,' I explained.

'You're not doing the operations?'

I shook my head and smiled at him. I hoped it might reassure him.

'Well, you'd better get on with it,' he said, after a moment's silence. 'What did you want to ask me?'

I edged forward and sat down timidly on the chair beside his bed, taking out the notebook I kept in my pocket. Then I began working my way through the system of questions I'd been taught by Dr Taylor and which are designed for use with surgical as well as with medical patients.

After half an hour I'd acquired not one neat diagnosis but three. And that, I knew, just wouldn't do at all. All young students are taught that, when interviewing a patient, they should attempt to tie all the information they acquire into one neat bundle and then stick a single diagnostic label on to the result.

For example, if a patient complains of a headache, a pain in his back, aches in his legs, a cough and a feeling of nausea, there's a good chance that he has a virus infection. A patient who complains of pain when she passes urine and also has pain in her loins is likely to have a kidney infection. And one who complains of an intolerance to fatty foods, a tendency to sickness, a pain in the right side of the abdomen and perhaps in the right shoulder, and a darkening of the urine is likely to find herself lying, like Mrs Potter, on the operating-table and having her gall bladder removed.

Mr Tucker's story just didn't lead to one answer. He told me that he had a swelling in his groin which got bigger when he coughed, a habit of getting up at night to urinate, a poor stream of urine when he did go, and difficulty in starting or stopping the flow. He also reported that he got pains in the upper part of his abdomen when he ate anything and that at night, when he wasn't being woken by the desire to micturate, he often woke up with a pain in his stomach. Try as I might, I just could not make sense of that collection of miscellaneous symptoms. Moreover, by the end of my interrogation, my embarrassment had not unnaturally doubled. In fact I think it was beginning to affect my judgement.

As I sat staring at the collection of notes I'd made, Mr Grant appeared on the ward. Seeing me sitting by the side of my patient he came over to offer support, help or possibly just criticism.

'Well?'

'I think it's something very rare,' I said in a whisper.

The registrar looked surprised.

'I'm having a little difficulty in getting a diagnosis,' I confessed.

'That doesn't necessarily make it rare,' he pointed out.

I recited to him the list of positive findings I'd acquired from my interview with Mr Tucker.

'Have you examined him yet?' he asked. I had to admit that I hadn't. Looking rather ashen at the prospect, but hardly likely to have felt worse than I did, my former physics teacher began to unbutton his pyjama jacket. With Mr Grant watching from the other side of the bed I began the examination. I discovered nothing more telling than a slight swelling in my patient's left groin, which appeared only when he coughed.

'Have you completed your examination?' asked the registrar.

I said I had.

'What about the rectal examination?'

'I haven't done that,' I agreed. The thought of sticking a finger into Mr Tucker's anus didn't appeal to my imagination. But, of course, such feelings have no place in medicine.

Fetching a rubber glove and a tube of cream from the far end of the ward, I invited Mr Tucker to lie on his side and draw his knees up to his chest. Then, liberally smearing my forefinger with lubricant, I slid it out of sight between his surprisingly hairy buttocks. As I did so, to our mutual embarrassment Mr Grant's bleep began to sound the high-pitched note indicating that the hospital switchboard operator had a call for him. Mr Tucker and I, mistaking the sound, apologised to one another and I withdrew my finger. While the registrar ran down the ward to the telephone,

Mr Tucker pulled up his pyjama trousers and I removed the rubber glove. We grinned at each other like conspirators.

'Well?' said Mr Grant, hurrying back a moment later.

'He's got an enlarged prostate gland,' I said.

'And?'

'And a hernia.'

'And?'

'An ulcer?' I suggested tentatively.

'Right,' agreed Mr Grant. 'Nothing rare. Just an ulcer, a hernia and an enlarged prostate.' He pulled the sheets back up over Mr Tucker. 'Always look for the simple things,' he reminded me. 'The common things are commonest.'

Bewildered by the problem of satisfying both Mr Grant and those who had warned me always to try to give each patient one diagnosis, I hardly heard him tell me that he'd just had a telephone call from the sister on the woman's surgical ward.

'I don't suppose you know anything about that, do you?' he asked.

'Sorry,' I said. 'What was that?'

'Sister Beresford's just had a telephone call from Mrs Potter's husband,' he repeated. 'He's an industrial chemist and apparently he's been trying to analyse the stones we took out of Mrs Potter's gall bladder.' He looked straight at me. 'They won't dissolve.'

I opened my mouth but fortunately nothing came out of it.

'I don't suppose you can explain that, can you?'

I told him it seemed a real mystery.

Chapter Fourteen

The university of which St Peter's Medical School was a part provided courses for several thousand people. There were engineering students, law students, students studying the social sciences, language students, history students, biology students, philosophers, mathematicians and so on. In all, there were approximately 20,000 people living, working, reading and — it was to be hoped — learning on the campus. Not all of them students, of course.

To provide all these students, lecturers, cleaners, laboratory technicians, professors, housekeepers, clerks, demonstrators and administrators with information about university affairs, a university newspaper was published once a week during term-time. It contained the usual mixture of gossip, political argument, domestic chit-chat and advance publicity for officially organised dances and theatrical events.

Andrew, my flat-mate, had early in his clinical career been appointed medical school correspondent for the newspaper. Most of the printed news comprised details of unusual academic successes and notices of new appointments within the faculty, but there was also the odd exposé. Occasionally Andrew reported on clinical research work which he considered important enough to merit a wider audience.

Because of his contacts among the newspaper's editorial staff, he knew far more non-medical students than any of my other friends. He was on nodding terms with historians, chemical engineers and English language students, and could even tell the difference between a pure and an applied mathematician.

Once a month the newspaper organised a dance and party in the main university hall. It was from the profits made at the bar at these dances that the paper managed to keep going; there was very little profit to be made from the sales. Indeed for five years the paper had made a steady loss, none of the students involved with its production ever having been enthusiastic about selling advertising space. During our attachment to Mr Meridew's surgical team, Andrew invited me to one of these dances. He was going with Sara. Since my romantic achievements (unless you count the night with Sister Henderson) had amounted to a kiss in the laundry room behind the main operating-theatre from a diminutive student nurse who seemed to regret it afterwards, I was ready for almost any opportunity.

To everyone's surprise the affair between Andrew and Sara had flourished; they seemed to grow together day by day. Those who had cruelly suggested that it was built on dubious needs, and therefore likely to founder, were beginning to agree that they'd been wrong in their assessment.

Only a couple of inches over five feet tall, and as slim and frail as a wraith, Sara worked as a typist for a firm of estate agents. Her father was a solicitor. His ambitions for his daughter had been largely academic, and had far exceeded Sara's own ambitions or intellectual capabilities. The pressures on her had been so great that at sixteen she'd attempted to put an end to it all with the help of a bottleful of aspirin tablets. The psychiatrist who'd seen her after the attempt had diagnosed schizophrenia, and tied the label to her without a second thought. As a result of that, Sara's parents had shied away from her, full of guilt and apprehension.

So thin that she always wore long-sleeved blouses to hide her bony arms and trousers to hide her legs, Sara had spent many months in a number of different mental hospitals, under the care of various psychiatrists. One had recommended electrical shock treatment, another had suggested surgery and others had simply tried different combinations of tranquillising drugs. None of these things had any beneficial effect and, when she and Andrew had met, Sara had been rapidly moving towards a state of institutionalisation: she was developing the dull, timid stare and manner of the long-term hospital patient who comes to accept every instruction and order with immediate obedience and to find life unbearable without strict regulation.

Hector had several times pointed out to anyone who

would listen to him that Andrew's infatuation was unhealthy for both Sara and himself, arguing that Sara was merely leaning on Andrew and that Andrew simply found it gratifying to have such a totally subservient and dependent companion. Slowly, however, it became apparent that Sara was developing a personality of her own and that Andrew was encouraging her to do so. A month after she'd left the mental hospital, Sara moved into Andrew's room in the flat. Her break with her parents had been precipitated by their dislike of Andrew, whom they felt too crude and rough a fellow for their daughter.

The three of us walked from the flat to the university hall together. On the way there we called in at the newspaper's editorial offices so that Andrew could get hold of a copy of the following day's paper, due in from the printers that same evening. The huge piles, bound with thick fraying string, were dumped in the narrow corridor outside the offices. Cutting the string on one pile, Andrew pulled out a couple of copies and handed one to me.

Instead of turning to the inside pages as he usually did, to see his small reports, invariably scattered among items delivered by correspondents from other faculties, Andrew spread out the front page.

'Look at that!' he whispered, pointing to the headline which stretched right across the paper. I put my copy down on one of the unopened bundles and simply stared at it. The front-page story described in extravagant detail the experiment which Andrew and I had helped Dr Taylor conduct. There was even a photograph of Mr Devlin and a number of quotes from an interview with Andrew. The screaming headline denounced both Dr Taylor and the Angipax research project, and the text detailed the agonies and terrors which Mr Devlin had endured in the cause of research.

'You can't print that,' I told him, my heart thumping and the butterflies in my stomach stamping around with leaden feet.

'I have,' he said, quite simply and proudly.

'But they'll never let you get away with it.'

‘What can they do? It’s all true.’

I read the story again. It described how Mr Devlin had been admitted to St Peter’s, how he’d been put on Angipax and how he’d been subjected to cardiac catheterisation several times after he’d been officially discharged from the hospital.

‘I still say those catheterisations were done because Dr Taylor was anxious to complete his research project,’ said Andrew, ‘and not for Devlin’s benefit.’

‘But they’ll say they got his permission,’ I exclaimed.

‘He didn’t understand what it was all about. Anyway, he was frightened by it all. He thought he had to do what they said.’

Nothing I said seemed to perturb Andrew at all; he was quite convinced that he was right and they were wrong. When my fears for his future had begun to settle I began to realise that I now had another problem to sort out, another moral quandary to solve. I just didn’t know whether or not Andrew was right; whether or not Mr Devlin had been treated properly and if he had been used by the medical system for its own ends rather than for his own good.

With all that on my mind, the dance was far from a success. I spent the evening with a student from the teacher training college which adjoined the campus and often provided female fodder for the hungry male students. She was already developing the tell-tale signs of pedagogy, but she had a good figure and all the usual accoutrements. Unfortunately, when I tried to put the relationship on to a more informal basis she explained to me that she only allowed heavy petting on a third date. I went back to the flat alone and lay awake listening to the sound of Andrew’s bedsprings.

Chapter Fifteen

Mr Nicholas Blake, Parliamentary Under-Secretary at the Department of Health, had been moved to a surgical ward. Despite Professor Grainger's careful attention, the clot in his leg had succeeded in sending a small embolism into a lung, producing breathlessness in Mr Blake and a cold sweat in Professor Grainger.

Mr Meridew had been asked to consider operating, and had agreed to see the politician only on condition that he allows himself to be treated on a public ward and made available for teaching purposes. Mr Meridew and Mr Blake had little in common, and certainly did not share any political beliefs. But the surgeon argued vociferously that a socialist politician should enjoy the same medical facilities as all his fellow-citizens and not expect private treatment. When Mr Blake demurred, Mr Meridew not only threatened to refuse to assist in his case but also made it clear that he wouldn't be averse to making a press statement about Mr Blake's expectations. That did it, and Mr Blake appeared within an hour on the male surgical ward, sitting in a bed less than three yards away from Mr Tucker. Between them lay a ninety-six-year-old man with an annoying habit of throwing his urine-bottle at anyone who approached. Mr Meridew made no secret of the fact that he expected this to act as a deterrent, keeping away the continuous stream of aides, civil servants and advisers who'd previously trotted along to the politician's bedside.

An hour after Mr Blake's arrival another new patient was admitted. The house surgeon, a young man with a greater reputation for his skills with a rugby football than his prowess with a scalpel, was away from the hospital again preparing for an international match, and the surgical registrar told me to take a history from the patient, examine him and decide what needed doing.

'I keep getting this pain in my back,' complained the man, who was in his mid-thirties but had the body of a man in his mid-forties. He told me that the pain, in his loin, came and went without any obvious pattern. Not unlike Mr

Tucker, he also reported that he had difficulty in passing urine, pain when he did manage it and an embarrassing need to visit the lavatory far more frequently than usual.

I scribbled feverishly in my notebook as he told me all this. Then I hurried back down the ward to report to Mr Grant. It looked very much as if I'd made my first straightforward diagnosis on the surgical ward. Mr Lamb, who'd told me that he worked as a communications expert, had even reported that he'd passed a little blood in his urine, and offered the opinion that he thought he might have acquired a little stone or something around his kidney. Not being too proud to accept diagnoses offered to me by patients, I was quite ready to adopt this as my own conclusion.

In the sister's office Mr Grant was clearly feeling the pressure. Mr Blake's arrival on the ward had triggered off an enormous series of enquiries from representatives of the press. Two reporters from national newspapers had already appeared on the ward and been ordered away by the sister. The telephone had been ringing non-stop for over an hour.

Mr Grant was busy trying to tell the hospital administrator just what had happened to Mr Blake and why he was now under Mr Meridew's care. 'He had a deep vein thrombosis in his leg,' he explained for the fourth time, 'and Professor Grainger had started him off on an anticoagulant to try to reduce the clot and prevent any complications.'

'What exactly caused the thrombosis?' asked the administrator, writing carefully and painstakingly in a small black leather-bound notebook. He it was who would be preparing the statement for the press to be issued later.

'I don't know,' replied Grant. 'There are lots of possible causes. Does it really matter?'

'Of course it matters,' replied the administrator, shocked. 'May I remind you, Mr Grant, that this is the Parliamentary Under-Secretary we're talking about?'

'I still don't know what caused the clot! But, if the damned fool had listened to Professor Grainger, he'd still be stuck up there in his nice comfortable private room instead of causing bloody chaos down here.'

The administrator sighed and shook his head in dismay.

'Blake was told to rest,' said Mr Grant, 'but he was seen giving a press conference in the hospital corridor.'

'There's an industrial dispute developing in Wales.'

'Well, there's a nice big clot developed in his lung now.'

'I've just seen that new patient,' I interrupted cautiously. 'I think he's got renal colic.'

'Give him a hundred milligrams of pethidine,' Mr Grant ordered without even looking at me.

'I'm not entirely sure...' I said hesitantly.

'Well, what else do you think he could have?' asked Mr Grant, turning away from the administrator for a moment.

'With all these reporters...' I said, 'I wondered if he could be just trying to get hold of a good story...'

'Splendid!' laughed the registrar. 'That's all we needed.'

He pushed the hair back from his forehead and closed his eyes. 'Give him the pethidine anyway. If he's got colic he needs it, and if he's a reporter it'll keep him quiet.'

'Really!' said the administrator unhappily.

'Is that all you want to know?' the registrar asked him.

'What's the prognosis?' asked the administrator. 'When will he be able to leave the ward?'

'I don't know,' said Mr Grant bluntly. 'Mr Meridew is going to perform an embolectomy, to remove the clot from Mr Blake's lung.'

'Is this always successful?' asked the administrator, scribbling furiously.

'No operation is always successful. And this is riskier than most.'

The administrator paled and scribbled out whatever it was he'd just written. As he did so, and as I took a vial of pethidine from the ward sister, a cleaner shyly poked her head round the office door.

'Excuse me, sirs,' she said hesitantly, 'but there's an awful rumpus going on down on the ward.' She darted away immediately and I followed Mr Grant and the ward sister out of the office. The cleaner was right. Mr Blake was sitting up in bed beaming for two photographers who had somehow managed to get on to the ward.

'Get out of here!' Mr Grant shouted at them.

'Just a moment,' Mr Blake said, raising a finger in admonition. 'These gentlemen were just taking a few photographs for their newspapers. We must co-operate with the press, you know.' He had leant forward to shake hands with one of the photographers when he suddenly fell backwards, clutching his chest.

'Oh dear, oh dear,' cried the administrator, who'd followed us on to the ward and was now standing transfixed.

'Bloody hell,' said one of the photographers, taking two rapid pictures and running out of the ward. His colleague stayed for a few extra shots before racing after him.

'Shall I get theatre ready for him?' asked the sister.

Mr Grant shook his head. 'You can forget it. He's had an enormous clot. He won't be making any more speeches.'

He began to pull the curtains around the late Under-Secretary's bed. I reached up to help him and noticed the vial of pethidine in my hand.

'Would you have a look at Mr Lamb?' I asked him. 'The new patient with colic.'

He followed me to the man's bed and stared for a moment at the face before him. 'I know you, don't I?'

'I don't think so, doctor,' said the patient.

'Harbury General Hospital,' said Mr Grant suddenly. 'Last year. I was doing a locum there for the consultant surgeon.'

'Never been there,' said the patient quite definitely.

'Ken Lyons, isn't it?' said the registrar, grinning.

'This is Mr Lamb,' I pointed out. As I said it the connection struck me. I grinned, too.

'He's a pethidine addict,' said Mr Grant. 'Gets himself admitted as a case of renal colic and gets his injections that way.'

'That's not true!' complained the patient.

'You've got three minutes to get dressed and get out of this ward,' said Mr Grant. 'If you're not gone by then, I'll call the police.'

Miraculously Mr Lamb/Lyons suddenly found the strength to jump out of bed, dress and scurry off the ward.

The administrator, who'd still not moved, simply saw a patient running away from his bed, and began to look very ill.

Chapter Sixteen

The next few days were hectic. The death of the Parliamentary Under-Secretary kept us all busy answering questions. Even I was not able to escape the enquiry which inevitably followed. The hospital committee members who set it up wanted to know everything I'd seen and heard. Even when I explained that I knew very little of what had gone on they still seemed to think I was hiding something. They insisted on my answering questions for another hour.

Andrew had been having a hard time too. He'd spent two hours With the Dean of St Peter's Medical School and a further hour with the hospital's governors. They'd obviously been more than a little upset by the story in the university paper, but there had been little they could do about it without attracting more attention. In the end they'd settled for giving Andrew a good telling-off and extracting from him a written promise that anything else he wrote about the medical school would be cleared first of all with the Dean himself.

The result of all this confusion was that our formal medical education seemed to stumble to a halt. The new patients admitted to the male surgical ward were suffering from routine problems. One had piles which needed annihilating; another a cyst on his back which had been taken away six months previously, but obviously needed to be taken farther away, since it had recurred.

There was one new patient on the female ward who proved memorable for several reasons.

Mrs Doreen Rogers was admitted because she was overweight. She had varicose veins, piles and a hiatus hernia which gave her heartburn every time she came within spitting distance of her feet, but her main problem was simply her weight. Still in her twenties, she weighed 266 pounds and was beginning to suffer badly. Even when it was cool she found breathing difficult; when the weather was hot she found it nigh on impossible. She insisted that she ate nothing more than a moth needs to keep body and wings together, and her evidence was so convincing that I, at least, decided that medical scientists must know nothing at all about the metabolic processes dealing with fat, or the mechanisms which turn food into flesh.

She had come into hospital to have a few feet of bowel removed. Mr Meridew, an imaginative and innovative surgeon, had developed an operation which involved cutting out a length of intestine so that food travelling through had less chance to be absorbed; Mrs Rogers seemed an ideal candidate. It was rather a frightening operation, with considerable risks, but although the dangers had been explained to her Mrs Rogers was enthusiastic about it. She'd discovered that her husband had begun an affair with a neighbour and she was determined to win back his affection.

During the previous four or five months she had, so she claimed, really struggled to slim. She'd tried diets involving nothing more than grapefruit and radishes, she'd bought a rowing machine because she was too shy to be seen jogging in the streets, and she'd swallowed tablets by the pound. Unhappily she'd found herself unable to stop eating grapefruit and radishes in excessive quantities, so that she'd not only put on weight but had also produced an extraordinary amount of wind; she'd broken the rowing machine the first time she'd sat on it; and the tablets had simply filled her up with calorie-rich sugar coatings.

When I wasn't listening to her describing her painstaking attempts to reduce weight, I sat listening to Mr Tucker, who'd had his prostrate gland removed and lost his hernia.

He complained that in hospital he felt intimidated and emasculated, and wanted to know why he couldn't have his clothes back now that he was supposed to be convalescing, why he had to be woken at six with a cup of strong tea and why he wasn't allowed to go home and convalesce. He also complained that his shaven pubic area was itching and wanted to know what I could do about it. Our relationship was an unusual one. In my white coat I felt that I had some natural protection against such awkward questions. On the other hand, Mr Tucker had been my teacher for several years and he had the advantage of age. My façade of wisdom and medical dignity was still slight and easily penetrated.

Hector was far more confident. He spent every spare moment practising tying knots, and our flat was littered with short lengths of nylon and catgut. He'd already been promised a job as Mr Meridew's house surgeon, and was working hard on Dr Taylor in an attempt to assure himself of an appointment as house physician to the professor of medicine. His career was beginning to take shape. He'd even performed an appendicectomy on his own, with the eternally kind anaesthetist Jim Kibble-White offering advice and instruction from the head of the operating-table.

Hector had become engaged to a dietician, a relationship which had contributed considerably to the nutrition of both him and myself. Andrew and Sara were content to continue with a diet of meat pies, fried fish, chips and mushy peas, this being the variety available at the local fish and chip shop. Hector and I, however, were able to dine on woodpigeon, avocado pear, home-baked apple-pie, freshly made pizza, trout with almonds and bananas, Camembert cheese, roll-mop herrings and freshly prepared meringues. I never asked how Hector's dietician managed to produce such remarkable fare on a housekeeping budget of three pounds a week, but I suspect the fact that her father owned a restaurant in the city may have had some bearing on the matter.

After three days in hospital, Mrs Rogers began to complain of pains in her back and lower abdomen. Mr Meridew and Mr Grant examined her thoroughly but could find no explanation. Undoubtedly their diagnostic attempts were hindered by the fact that her flesh was so abundant that all her internal organs and structures were a good distance away from any investigating fingers.

That at least was the explanation offered by Mr Grant — until Mrs Rogers suddenly lost nearly thirty pounds in the space of an hour, and became the proud mother of two perfectly formed and well-fleshed sons.

Bedded as she was on a surgical ward, Mrs Rogers became a local celebrity. The nurses, delighted both by the enormousness of the error made by the surgeons and by the arrival of two charming and chuckling infants, made a tremendous fuss of her.

Mr Rogers, who'd arrived on the ward that day a reluctant and unfaithful husband, left a proud and contented father. Two days later his wife left hospital with her new offspring, abandoning (temporarily, at least) her intention to have surgery for her obesity. It was several weeks before Mr Meridew regained his former ebullience, and for several years afterwards all women of child-bearing age admitted to the women's surgical ward had a pregnancy test done as a matter of routine. Even a nun, admitted to have her thyroid gland removed, fell under suspicion.

It did at least all help to remove some of the gloom.

Chapter Seventeen

Suddenly, almost without our being aware of it at all, there were examinations to be taken. We'd all spent some time on the medical wards and some on the surgical wards, and in addition there had been short periods in specialist hospitals. I'd spent a few afternoons in an infectious diseases hospital where I'd seen a case of malaria, a patient with brucellosis and a girl with typhoid. I hadn't seen any cases of measles, chickenpox, German measles, scabies, syphilis, mumps or shingles. I'd spent an afternoon in the local dental hospital, but what I'd learnt about dentistry you could write with a felt-tip pen on a single artificial incisor. I'd stood for two whole mornings in an eye hospital and learnt how to switch on and off an ophthalmoscope. For a day I'd wandered round an ear, nose and throat hospital with a light-bulb and metal reflector strapped to my head, and for four hours I'd stood in an orthopaedics clinic at the local accident hospital where I'd watched sixty-four patients with plaster casts on various limbs parade before a weary registrar who had, apparently indiscriminately, given half of them a note to return to work and the other half a note to return to the clinic in a month's time.

I'd learnt about Whipples disease, the Waterhouse-Friderichsen syndrome, Pancoast's tumour, the Klippel-Feil deformity, Gilbert's disease, the Austin Flint heart murmur, the Brown Sequard syndrome, Libman Sachs endocarditis, the Kveim test, Kernig's sign, Stokes Adams attacks, Wolff-Parkinson-White syndrome, von Recklinghausen's disease, the Schilling test and Bence Jones proteins, as well as Charcot-Marie-Tooth disease, Chvostek's sign, and the difference between Huntington's and Sydenham's chorea. As you may imagine from this modest list, doctors rather like immortality, and attach their names to any new disease or sign they can identify.

Unfortunately, however, I knew far less about body lice, eczema, arthritis or food poisoning, since none of these subjects had attracted the attention of my teachers. Nor did I know a great deal about bed-wetting, insomnia, broken legs or anxiety.

The information I'd collected during my two hectic pre-clinical years was, despite my initial suspicions, proving to be of occasional use. I'd learnt the anatomy of the human body in excruciatingly minute detail and, although I'd long since forgotten most of it, there were still pockets of knowledge there to be tapped at unexpected moments. To help in the accumulation of anatomical facts all medical students use mnemonics, memory-aids which linger in the mind much longer than straightforward unassociated and intrinsically uninteresting facts. I could still recite the names of the structures which passed through the superior orbital fissure at the back of the eyeball by remembering that luscious French tarts lie naked in anticipation. To remember the names and numbers of the twelve cranial nerves, which supply the structures in and around the skull, I had only to recall the sentence, 'Oh, oh, Oswald, to touch and fondle a girl's vagina and hymen'. This moderately obscene memory-aid told me that the first cranial nerve is the olfactory nerve, the second the optic and the third the oculomotor. Those which follow are the trochlear, the trigeminal, the abducent, the facial, the auditory, the glossopharyngeal, the vagus, the accessory and the hyoglossal. I dare say some elderly ladies may well be surprised to discover that their sweet and charming family doctor first learnt his anatomy with the aid of such outrageous nonsense.

True, I had yet to meet a patient whose clinical problems required knowledge either of the structures passing through the superior orbital fissure, or of the names of the cranial nerves, but the knowledge was there, waiting to be used. Which is more than can be said of information about the drug treatment of patients. Despite the fact that as a qualified doctor most of my treatments would, unless I chose to specialise as a surgeon, involve the use of drugs, I'd received very little training in their selection and use. We'd received a few desultory lectures from a pharmacologist, dealing with the chemical structure of certain specific drugs, and we'd seen a film describing the manufacturing process used in the preparation of tablets, but we'd had no training at all in prescription. I felt this ignorance keenly and had several times floundered through the pages of pharmacological textbooks in search of advice. I might as well have struggled to learn neurosurgery by mail.

I could now take blood from most of the patients I encountered without having to cry for help, and I could put sutures into small wounds and tie knots that held together for hours rather than minutes — both these skills having been acquired while practising on unconscious patients on the operating-table. If the patients had seen my fumbling fingers, they'd undoubtedly have preferred to do the work themselves. I'd explored the inner recesses of both male and female patients, and seen enough to be aware that things aren't always what they seem to be. Andrew had once examined a woman with a capacious vagina and been quite unable to find her cervix. The gynaecologist looking after her had then discovered that for eighteen years her husband had used her urethra as a repository for his penis. This error explained both her incontinence and their lack of progeny.

I could elicit knee reflexes, hear the louder murmurs of malfunctioning hearts, tie my surgical mask on without help, ask embarrassing questions without blushing, recognise a malar flush, examine a shapely breast without the sound of my heart waking patients in the next ward, list twelve possible causes of anaemia and find the spleen in at least half of the patients described by the registrars as having palpable spleens.

I was becoming a doctor. I no longer lay awake at night worrying about poor Mrs Kennedy, who had killed herself. I could walk away from a cadaver and go straight to the next patient. And I could watch a surgeon remove an arm or a leg without feeling faint. I still felt a rush of anger when I heard other students refer to patients as 'the gall bladder in the end bed' or the 'lump in the fourth bed along', but I no longer felt self-conscious when I walked on to the ward at visiting-time.

On the other hand I still often wanted to talk to patients as a friend rather than as a doctor. I felt uncomfortable when they opened up their hearts to me while I couldn't open up mine to them. And occasionally I envied veterinary surgeons, who know that their patients never tell them lies and can rely on the information they receive. I also envied them their ability, even duty, to put a patient doomed to a painful death out of his misery. The vet who allowed an animal to die a slow and painful death would be reviled. The doctor is expected to do nothing to interfere with nature when death is inevitable, although he may, of course, provide pain-relief and some support.

The examinations came and went within a week. There were patients to be examined, written papers to do, vivas to attend. And suddenly I was on the home stretch. Just one more hurdle — finals — lay before me and then I'd be a qualified medical practitioner. There was so much to be learnt in that year — so much that I knew it was quite impossible. How could anyone learn enough in less than a hundred years to qualify as a doctor? I had so little time and so much to learn.

Chapter Eighteen

I began my last lap at medical school by working at the Kintbury General Hospital for a month. Like many busy hospitals, the Kintbury General, which was five miles from St Peter's in purely geographical terms but a half a century away in technological terms, was permanently short of qualified doctors. The sudden departure of a Greek-speaking house physician who'd inexplicably decided that a 120-hour week was too much for him had left the hospital poised perilously close to disaster. So close, in fact, that for the fourth time in as many months the Kintbury General had begged the medical school for the loan of a senior medical student to act as a locum until a replacement doctor could be found. I happened to be standing in the corridor outside the Dean's office when the call came through, and I found myself being invited to accept this temporary appointment. The fact that the invitation was an instruction, and that I had been chosen simply and solely because I had a date with a typist from the Assistant Dean's administrative office, didn't detract from the elation I felt at this temporary elevation to the ranks of the immortals. I abandoned my tryst and hurried back to the flat to pack a bag.

My first problem was the simple one of actually finding the Kintbury General. Previous expeditions away from St Peter's had been confined to visits to the cinema, the main railway station and the other specialist hospitals where I had worked or studied. On the days when I'd been unable to cadge a lift from some other student who could afford a car, I'd travelled on bus routes carefully described to me in advance by one of the switchboard operators at St Peter's.

Unhappily that source of information was on holiday in Torremolinos, and I had to find my own way. Suppressing the inclination to follow Andrew's advice and simply lie down in the road, feign unconsciousness and trust to luck that I'd be taken to the Kintbury General, I spent the next two and a half hours standing in the rain waiting for buses, sitting on buses anxiously peering into the gloom, and getting off buses, retracing my steps on foot and asking an astonishing number of foreigners if they could help me with practical advice. Sheltering in a telephone kiosk from a particularly heavy shower, I telephoned the girl from the Assistant Dean's office, thinking that I ought perhaps to make some apology for my failure to keep our date. It turned out that she lived with her parents about two hundred yards away from the hospital I was searching for, and she found the irony more amusing than I did.

Eventually, of course, I found it. No husband hurrying with his labouring wife has ever breathed deeper sighs of relief. The ancient dark brick turrets and the modern semi-luminous green and white signs seemed almost welcoming. The night was getting no younger, my stomach was getting no fuller and my feet were getting wetter and colder. I began to dream of huge platefuls of steaming hot food: steak and kidney pie and apple crumble perhaps. Or maybe a large bowl of tomato soup, a plateful of cod and chips and some treacle pudding. Certainly at least three large cups of black coffee and, if the doctors' mess was open, maybe even a half-pint of beer to round off the meal. My room would, I knew by now, be no better than the other hospital rooms I'd slept in, but at least the sheets would be crisp and clean. My bedding in the flat was rather overdue for washing, and it would be a distinct pleasure to slide between wrinkle-free sheets.

It didn't quite work out like that, of course. The hospital had been allowed to grow over several decades and no single mind had ever controlled its growth. With facilities for several hundred patients spread among several dozen separate buildings, it was no easy matter to find the correct part, and extremely difficult to find the right person to report to. In the administrative block there wasn't a soul to be found. Only the occasional thump from the cooling radiators confirmed that the place had ever been inhabited. The lights had all been switched off and, as I blundered around, the shadows grew spookier and spookier. My tiny pencil-sized torch lit up only tiny areas of floor at a time and left plenty of room for my imagination to work overtime. So empty was it all that I walked round each corner half-expecting to find some giant monster gobbling up the last remaining clerical officer or to see a wild-eyed bacteriologist rush past me with an empty test-tube in pursuit of an escaped bacterium. I could imagine the patients running away if they knew I was coming, but what had the administrative staff to fear? And where were all the nurses and doctors? Was I the only person in the place? In a cupboard in a small kitchen I found a three-quarters-empty bottle of milk which smelt rancid, a packet of stale biscuits and a lemon-squash bottle containing an inch of heavily watered fluid. I drank the lemon squash and ate three of the biscuits.

Eventually I did what I should have done to start with. I followed the signs to the casualty department. There were plenty of bright shining lights there, and a pair of flashing ambulances complete with loudly blaring short-wave radios were parked outside the doors.

Inside, business was as brisk as it always seems to be in any casualty department. Two ambulancemen were helping two nurses hold down a struggling, shouting man who was clearly having some sort of fit. A doctor with a polo-necked sweater and a pair of green velvet trousers on underneath his white coat was calmly drawing up fluid into a syringe and talking to a third nurse who stood next to him with a small kidney dish containing some methylated spirit and half a dozen cotton-wool balls.

I waited until the injection had been given and the patient had stopped thrashing around, then timidly approached the doctor. I asked him where the doctors' mess was. When he looked puzzled I explained that I was a medical student and that I'd been sent to help out. As I said it, I realised just how totally pointless the whole exercise was. How could I possibly help anyone out?

'Great,' he said, rubbing his hands. 'This is Sister Watkins,' he went on, introducing me to the nurse who'd been helping him with the injection. Unlike the sisters at St Peter's she wore a green uniform; they all wore blue.

'I'll get you a white coat,' she said.

'It can wait until morning,' I replied, trying to be helpful. It didn't seem an urgent problem.

‘You’d better have one now,’ said the sister. ‘It’ll protect your clothes, and at least the patients will know who the doctor is.’ She smiled. I still didn’t properly understand. As she moved off to fetch me a white coat, I turned round to ask the casualty officer if he could tell me whether the doctors’ dining-room was still open. The question never got asked; he’d disappeared. It turned out that he’d gone to eat and I’d been left in charge of the casualty department.

I had no time at all to protest, for I’d hardly put down my small bag when there was a great commotion near the entrance. A new patient was brought in, not by ambulance men as I’d expected but two burly policemen and a small, extremely fragile-looking policewoman who provided vocal support and turned out to have an extensive vocabulary. The patient was covered in blood, as were the two policemen, and around his neck was tied a piece of electrical wire. From the noose there dangled about a yard and a half of free flex.

‘Suicide attempt,’ explained one of the policemen wearily.

‘Found him hanging from the top of the stairs in a pub.’

‘The flex had stretched,’ explained the second policeman, ‘and his feet were on the ground.’

‘He couldn’t undo the knot,’ said the first, ‘and couldn’t reach a knife.’

‘Threw a bottle out of the front-door window and hit an old gentleman on the ankle,’ said the second.

It was coming to sound like a script for Tweedledum and Tweedledee. The unfortunate patient, a Birmingham-born Indian who had a startling Midland accent, had cut his wrists before trying to hang himself, and the blood which smeared the two policemen as well as himself came from those cuts. Fortunately, neither radial artery had been severed, and the blood-loss, although considerable enough to cause some concern and a great deal of mess, wasn’t enough to threaten his life. His neck contained evidence of several attempts to cut the jugular veins or carotid arteries, with scratch-marks running right across from ear to ear.

While the sister cleaned his wrists and one of the policemen removed the noose from around his neck with the aid of a pair of plaster-cutting shears, I looked at the cuts which I had to suture. They were both about an inch long and needing two or three stitches. It was the sort of job any half-competent casualty officer would expect to do in ten or fifteen minutes. Fortunately, after the arrival of this patient the department was relatively quiet for the next hour and a half, for it took me that long to complete these minor surgical procedures. The patient and I got to know each other quite well.

It transpired that his wife had been in hospital for nine months, dying of breast cancer. She'd been treated by drugs, radiotherapy and surgery, having had her ovaries removed and her pituitary gland obliterated.

'It was funny,' said the man, his eyes dry but full of sadness. 'The house was never empty until she died. Somehow it didn't seem so bad until they told me she was dead.'

He'd gone along to the pub to drink away his sorrow, but had discovered that there was too much of it for alcohol to drown. The suicide attempt had followed almost as a matter of course. First the attempt to cut his throat, then the slash at his wrists and finally the abortive attempt to hang himself.

'I can't do anything properly,' said the man plaintively. 'Why are you wasting time on me, doctor?'

I talked to him as I stitched away, trying to understand the depth of his despair. But the deeper I dug the greater seemed the sorrow.

'We'll have to keep him in hospital,' I told the sister when at last I'd finished.

'Where?'

'On a ward,' I answered innocently. 'How do we organise that?'

The sister explained that first of all we had to find a consultant willing to look after him and a ward with a bed for him. And so began one of the strangest interludes of my young medical career. First I rang the medical registrar, who was at home half a mile from the hospital. When I explained that the patient had tried to commit suicide, he told me that I'd have to get in touch with the psychiatrists. The consultant psychiatrist I spoke to at home wasn't interested.

'Cut his wrists, you say?' he commented. 'That's a surgical problem.'

'But he's very depressed,' I pointed out. 'He may try again.'

'We'll have a look at him when his cuts have healed up,' promised the psychiatrist. 'Try the surgeons.'

The surgical registrar at the Kintbury General was off duty and couldn't be found anywhere. The house surgeon was busy putting up a drip and couldn't be disturbed and, when I telephoned the consultant surgeon to ask if he'd have on one of his wards a patient who had cut his wrists, I discovered that the policewoman's command of the vernacular was modest indeed when compared with the consultant surgeon's.

'How old is he?' he asked, before I put down the telephone.

'Forty-six,' I replied.

'Pity,' said the surgeon. 'Twenty years older and you could have tried the geriatricians.'

While the patient lay on the operating-table and I sat by the telephone with my head in my hands, wondering if the gynaecologists could be persuaded to take the man on the grounds that his wife had once been on one of their wards, the two policemen and the policewoman who had brought him in arrived back. They'd disappeared as I'd finished sewing up the man's first wound. With them they brought two young children, one aged six and the other eight. They both had bad colds and sniffed continuously.

'Someone at the pub told us about the children,' said the policewoman with gruff kindliness. 'We found them sitting watching a blank television screen at their home.'

'What have you brought them here for?' asked the casualty sister.

'There's nowhere else to take them. We can't get hold of a social worker until the morning.'

Picking up the telephone, inspired by desperation more than by sense, I asked the operator to connect me to the paediatrician.

‘I’ve got two young patients for you,’ I told him. ‘Both got upper respiratory tract infections.’

To my surprise the paediatrician didn’t argue for a moment.

‘Send them along,’ he groaned sleepily.

‘One other thing,’ I said, before he hung up. ‘Have you got a bed for their father?’

‘Yeah,’ sighed the paediatrician. ‘Send him up, too.’

And so I sent my unfortunate Indian to the children’s ward, where he and his two children were bedded down for the night. The casualty sister telephoned the sister on the children’s ward and arranged for their father to be given an injection of a sedative drug for the night. It all seemed rather odd, but at least we’d managed to find him a bed.

As a porter trundled off with my neatly mended patient and his offspring, I remembered that I still hadn’t eaten.

Hesitantly I mentioned it to the casualty sister.

‘That’s all right,’ she said, with a reassuring smile. ‘You go along to the nurses’ canteen. The doctors’ dining-room is closed now.’

‘Will it be, er...?’ I asked. ‘Will it be all right? Are you sure? What if something happens? An emergency or something?’

‘We’ll try to cope until we can get you or Dr Coleman here,’ she assured me. Dr Coleman was, I assumed, the casualty officer who’d been on duty when I’d arrived and who’d subsequently completely disappeared. I discovered the next day that he’d just gone back to bed, relying on the sister to call him if he were needed.

Wearily I took off my white coat and picked up my bag. The sister told me where to find the Canteen, and suggested that I call in at the doctors’ residence on the way, to find my room and drop my bag.

It was just as well I did so. The front door to the small wooden hut which was home for the residential medical staff was kept locked, but I got there as the house surgeon returned from putting the drip up, and he let me in.

‘You’d better have this room,’ he sighed, tiredly showing me a typical small hospital room furnished with chipped, yellowing functional woodwork. On the bedside table was a small brown envelope containing two keys, one for the room and one for the front door. The bed wasn't made up, but a pile of sheets and blankets was neatly folded at its foot.

Pausing only to throw them over it and put the keys in my pocket, I hurried off to the canteen. My stomach was beginning to play tunes, I was so hungry.

'We haven't got much choice, love,' said the lady there. 'There never is at this time of night.'

Those were accurate words. I dined off two chocolate éclairs and a gooseberry yoghurt, washed down with a cup of lukewarm hospital tea, upon the surface of which there floated a veritable squadron of tea-leaves. When I'd finished, the canteen lady read the leaves and told me that the weather was going to be cold and wet, and that I'd be lucky in love and unlucky at cards.

Chapter Nineteen

I seemed hardly to have got to sleep when I was woken by a woman in a green overall thrusting a cup of tea under my nose. Waking up in the morning has never been one of my strong points: I prefer to break myself into the day gently, lying in bed for a few moments to get the general feel of things and then slowly pottering around picking up bits and pieces of clothing. After about half an hour or so of this I'm usually ready to start thinking of shaving and beginning the usual early-morning chores. Breakfast is not something to be thrust without warning on to an empty stomach which hasn't had time to yawn and get its bearings.

It seemed they did things differently at the Kintbury General Hospital. The woman in the green overall had brought with her two starch-crisp white coats which she stood up at one end of the bed. With the cup of tea there were three small, grey biscuits.

'Breakfast in ten minutes, love,' she said. 'Bacon, egg and sausage; bacon and egg; sausage and egg; sausage and bacon; poached egg; scrambled egg or boiled.'

I blinked and moved cautiously.

'For breakfast,' she explained. 'What do you want? Any fried bread? We haven't got any tomatoes.'

'Just coffee and toast, please,' I mumbled. 'I'll be along in a few minutes.'

She backed away from me cautiously and fumbled behind her for the door-knob. She disappeared in an instant. Cautiously I sat up. The curtains had been opened, and outside it was pouring with rain.

By the time I'd washed, dressed and discovered without any shadow of doubt that I'd left my razor behind, the tea was cold. I poured it carefully down the sink and threw the biscuits out of the window. They landed in a large puddle and began slowly to float away. A bedraggled-looking sparrow pecked at one of them for a few seconds, but made no progress, and flew off in disgust.

The dining-room was small and cosy. The only person there was the casualty officer I'd met the previous evening.

He introduced himself at Dr Coleman and told me that he was the only resident house officer.

'There's a ward-round in three minutes,' he warned me, as I poured out a cup of thick black coffee and smeared marmalade over a piece of thick black toast. 'Dr Younger — that's the consultant — doesn't much like us being late, though he's a decent enough fellow.'

I gulped down a mouthful of coffee and took a bite out of the toast.

'You'll find that things are rather different here from St Peter's.'

I washed down the toast with a second huge gulp of coffee.

'We don't have any fancy equipment here. Most of our stuff comes from Oxfam.'

I looked at him and decided he was only partly joking.

'Still, there are advantages. Quite a lot of our patients actually get better and go home.'

I pushed the remains of the toast into my mouth.

'Well,' he said, standing up. 'If you've finished, we'd better make a move.'

To get from the doctors' residence to the hospital we had to run across the car-park. By the time we'd reached the security of the main building I was soaked, although Dr Coleman, who'd somehow managed to cover his head with the tail of his white coat, seemed quite dry. Tall, thin and untidy, he had hollow cheeks and dark pouches under his eyes. He looked quite ill; rather like pictures I'd seen of nineteenth-century poets with consumption.

Dr Younger had already started his round, and looked over his spectacles at us with something between distaste and relief. Since no consultant physician would ever dream of moving about inside a hospital without at least one other doctor, he had with him his registrar, a minute fellow with a broad, beaming smile, a coat that reached down to his ankles, and skin the colour of my breakfast toast.

'Good morning,' said Dr Younger, very carefully. He studied his watch for a few moments then stared at both of us in turn quite closely. When he looked at me he rubbed his chin thoughtfully. I introduced myself, explained that I was a medical student and apologised for being late. He said nothing, but rubbed at his chin again.

'You're not growing a beard, are you?' he asked me at last.

'No,' I promised. 'I forgot my razor.'

'Ah,' he said. 'Good.' He carried on examining the patient he'd been talking to when we'd arrived. It was a young man who'd apparently been admitted with a pneumothorax — a pocket of air in the chest cavity — and who was clearly making a good recovery. His bedside locker was piled high with magazines which contained colour photographs of young ladies. While Dr Younger listened to his chest Dr Coleman examined one of the magazines.

'Of course,' said Dr Younger, putting his stethoscope back into his pocket suddenly and moving away from the patient, 'we don't have a lot of expensive equipment here, you know. Not like your teaching hospital.'

I shook my head. It seemed as if everyone was anxious to justify the state of the hospital.

'By the time we can afford anything exotic here it'll be too expensive for us,' he went on. 'Still,' he sighed, 'whenever they get any new equipment at St Peter's the number of people suddenly requiring extra investigation or treatment goes up overnight. You'd think no one had survived until they had their new whatever-it-is. Well, we don't have time for fancy stuff like that here.'

'No, sir,' I agreed.

'These centres of excellence — teaching hospitals and so on — they're all right. But it's in our small local hospitals that all the really important work is done.' He stopped and turned round to make sure I was listening.

I nodded.

'We get our patients in and out,' he explained. 'There's no keeping people in just to take photographs of them or try out something new and fancy.'

I shook my head.

'It's all real solid medicine.' He took out his stethoscope and approached the next patient, a middle-aged man busily adding the finishing touches to a painting of a London scene which showed two weary-looking horses dragging a stage coach through a blizzard with the mail. Only when I looked very closely at it could I see the numbers showing through.

'Now, you take that fellow,' said Dr Younger, having listened to the man's chest and admired his painting. 'In your hospital, he'd have been wrapped up in all sorts of electrical wires and nonsense. He's had a coronary and he's doing very nicely, thank you, here.'

I'm afraid, however, that, although Dr Younger went on even longer, explaining to me just how well they'd coped with the heart-attack patient using such primitive methods of treatment as morphine and digitalis, I heard hardly anything of what he said. I was staring at the patient in the next bed — an elderly man whom I felt certain I recognised. Then, just as Dr Younger began to describe how he remembered leeches having been used to help reduce swellings caused by all sorts of strange disorders, I recalled where I'd seen the patient before. It was Mr Kennedy, the old man whose wife had been on Professor Grainger's first ward-round.

'How is this fellow?' Dr Younger asked, as we left the amateur artist and approached Mr Kennedy's bed.

'Still not speaking,' said the registrar, who continued to smile whatever the news he had to give. Later I saw him smiling as he told a middle-aged woman that her young son had been killed in a road accident. It wasn't that he meant anything disrespectful; it was just that he always smiled. His name was unpronounceable, but we all called him Sid, and the nurses and orderlies referred to him as Dr Sid. 'The speech therapists are coming in to see him today and the physiotherapists are still working on him.'

'This fellow has had a stroke,' Dr Younger explained to me. 'His wife committed suicide and tried to do away with her husband. She was lucky, but he lived. He was in St Peter's for a time.'

'I remember him,' I said quietly.

'Well, did you know what happened to him after that?' asked Dr Younger.

'No.'

'He was discharged from there and sent to an old people's home, where he promptly had a stroke. They wouldn't have him back at St Peter's, of course. They don't take problems like that there. So we've got him here. He's been with us for weeks now and looks like staying for a good few more. The geriatricians have a waiting-list so long that I think they run a ballot for emergency admissions. You stand a better chance of getting two stand-tickets for the Cup Final.'

'How's he doing?' I asked. 'Has he improved at all?'

'Has he?' Dr Younger asked Dr Sid.

The registrar shrugged his shoulders. 'Difficult to say,' he said. 'Some days he seems a bit brighter.' He looked across at Mr Kennedy, his beaming smile firmly in place. 'Sister says that yesterday he sat up by himself. He could be making some progress.'

We all moved on to the next patient. This time it was a man with a bad attack of pneumonia who'd been having six-hourly injections into his buttocks. He was anxious to leave, and Dr Younger was cheered by that. He explained that he could never get his beds emptied quickly enough.

'There's a tremendous pressure on them,' he explained. 'We have to look after the real cases,' he said acidly. 'We can't afford just to be choosy. When there's any problem requiring medical attention in our catchment area, we have to be available to take it in. And filling the beds with long-stay patients just means that we have to put up other beds in the corridors.'

Just then his bleep began to scream.

'Dear me,' he said, clapping his hand across it to drown the noise. 'Go and see what this is, will you?' I hurried back down the ward and asked the sister how I should find out who wanted Dr Younger. She picked up the telephone and handed it to me.

'It's his personal secretary,' said the operator. 'She says he's urgently needed for a domiciliary visit.'

I returned and gave him the message. He seemed upset but rushed off nevertheless.

'Right,' said Dr Coleman, when he'd gone. 'Now that the

boss has gone off to his football match, we can get some of these new patients clerked. Thank heavens for Manchester United.'

My puzzlement must have shown.

'He's a Manchester United fan,' explained Dr Coleman.

'They're playing the local team, so he'll be off to watch them.'

'But what about the urgent domiciliary visit?'

'Oh, that's just a little white lie to keep us all happy. He thinks we believe it. Or perhaps he doesn't. Perhaps he just thinks it makes everyone feel better about it. Or perhaps he does it to make himself feel better.' He scratched his head and shrugged.

'How many new patients have we got this morning?' asked Dr Sid. I still found his continuous smile disconcerting.

'Three,' said Dr Coleman. 'One each.' He looked across at me. 'What do you want?' he asked. 'A seventy-year-old with a bleeding ulcer, a nineteen-year-old with anaemia or a forty-five-year-old with chest pains.'

I told him that I thought I might be best able to cope with the nineteen-year-old. I couldn't have been farther from the truth.

Chapter Twenty

At first it looked as though I'd picked the right patient. Pale and delicate as a piece of Irish lace, she lay in bed with her arms straight out in front of her on top of the neatly folded sheets. Around her shoulders she wore a pale-blue knitted bedjacket and, underneath that, a modest nightdress which tied demurely about her neck. She wore her hair in an old-fashioned pony-tail, and her only make-up was a thin layer of lipstick. On her bedside locker were a copy of *Woman's Own*, Jerome K. Jerome's masterpiece *Three Men in a Boat* and a brown paper bag full of apples. Her name was Ellen Richards.

'Fine,' she said, when I asked her how she felt.

'No,' she told me, when I wanted to know if she had any pain.

It turned out that she'd first visited her family doctor two weeks before. She'd had a sore throat and was feeling rather tired. Her doctor had prescribed a course of penicillin and told her to come back in a week if she felt no better. A week later she'd returned; her sore throat was slightly better, but she was nonetheless still tired. The doctor, with great perception, had sent her for a blood test. It had shown that she was extremely anaemic, and the result had been her arrival at the Kintbury General.

'The throat's a lot better,' she told me. 'My doctor gave me another course of antibiotics and that helped clear it up.'

'So you're just feeling tired?'

She nodded.

I asked her if she got breathless.

'Not while I'm lying in bed,' she said, 'but I do if I try moving about much.'

And that was about all I could get from talking to her. I couldn't really understand what she was doing filling a hospital bed.

When I came to examine her I found little more to help me to a diagnosis. She had a few swollen glands in her neck and armpits but glands commonly enlarge after a bad throat infection. She was obviously anaemic, and there was no obvious explanation; but that, too, isn't uncommon.

'I don't know why they've brought me into hospital,' she said with a smile. 'I thought perhaps my doctor would just give me some iron tablets when he found out I was anaemic.'

'Well, we'll probably get you out soon,' I promised. We shook hands and I noticed how cold her hand was. She really did look rather frail.

I wrote up my admission notes in the ward sister's office on the official hospital notepaper used for such formal records. When I'd finished I clipped them into one of the beige cardboard folders stored in the desk drawer and wrote Ellen Richards' name on it. Then I went round to the men's medical ward to take another look at Mr Kennedy.

He was lying in exactly the same position, staring straight ahead and apparently studying carefully a laundry trolley which had been left abandoned in the central aisle of the ward.

'Do you remember me?' I asked him quietly. 'We met at St Peter's.'

Very slowly he turned his head to look at me. His eyes, which had been glazed and expressionless, very faintly showed some interest. He frowned as if concentrating hard, and then nodded. It was almost imperceptible, but it was a nod.

'Can you move your hand?' I asked him, touching the back of his right hand.

Nothing happened.

I lifted the hand a few inches off the bedclothes and then very gradually took my own fingers away. His hand remained where it was. Clearly he had some power in the muscles of his right arm.

'Put it down,' I told him. 'Put it back on the bed.'

Very slowly, again almost invisibly, Mr Kennedy lowered his hand back on to the bedclothes.

'Can you squeeze my fingers?' I put two fingers inside his palm. For a few seconds nothing happened, and then, very cautiously, he began to squeeze them. I leant forward excitedly and picked up his left arm.

‘Can you lift this arm up? ‘I asked him, very gently disentangling my fingers from his right hand.

This time he did so quite quickly. Then, slowly, he showed me that he could raise or lower it, and could squeeze my fingers quite efficiently.

‘Can you see?’ I asked him. ‘Squeeze twice if you can.’ I kept my fingers inside his left hand.

He nodded and then squeezed. Then he turned his head back towards me, and I could see tears forming in both eyes.

‘Can you read?’ I asked, thinking that perhaps I could fetch him a book, a paper or a magazine.

He shook his head. That confused me. He could see but he couldn’t read.

‘Is your sight bad?’

He nodded.

‘Do you wear spectacles?’

Another nod.

I rummaged around in the bedside locker. There were all sorts of things there. A suit of clothes, together with a leather belt and a pair of heavy working-boots, was placed neatly on top of an old grey raincoat which didn’t seem to have any buttons on it. I found Mr Kennedy’s spectacles inside a well-worn steel spectacle-case. I took them out, gave them a polish on a corner of my white coat and fitted them on to the bridge of his nose. I felt certain I’d solved his problem.

‘How is that?’ I asked. ‘Can you see better?’

When he shook his head I felt my spirits drop. I sat with him for several minutes more, just thinking. Then I had another idea.

‘Can you see double?’

He nodded, this time quite vigorously.

‘Is that what stops you reading?’ Another nod.

I took his spectacles off, tore a sheet of paper from my notepad and fixed it over one of the lenses. I put the spectacles back on his nose.

This time there was no need to ask if there was any improvement. He smiled, and his right hand groped tentatively out for mine. I bent down, fished an old newspaper out of the locker and held it in front of him. 'Can you read this?'

Mr Kennedy, with tears pouring down his cheeks, nodded, not just once but several times. I gripped his hand tightly and felt like crying with him. If I'm to be honest — and I have tried to be honest in this account from the beginning — then I have to admit that I felt very proud of myself.

Leaving him studying the cartoon page of a three-day-old daily newspaper, I hurried back across to the doctors' residence. It was ten past one and, according to the yellowing and tattered printed notice pasted on the back of my wardrobe door, lunch was served at one o'clock precisely. When I arrived in the dining-room it was deserted. I sat for a few moments studying the pattern of gravy stains on the tablecloth before finally plucking up the courage to jingle a few items of cutlery together. As I'd hoped, the noise brought a white-uniformed lady into the room. She had grey hair, rinsed in blue, and a series of chins which shook gently as she moved. She moved slowly around the table and flicked at the tablecloth with a rather dirty tea-towel.

Early in my career as a medical student — during my first week on the wards, in fact — I had learnt to play the diagnostic game when travelling on trains or buses or standing in shop queues. Many diseases can be recognised from a distance by using such pointers as facial colour, physiognomy, tics, hair colour or form, skin condition, gait, eye disorders and habits. The blank stare of Parkinson's disease, the stamping gait of advanced syphilis, the pallor of anaemia, the yellowy hue of a liver infection, the emaciation associated with a cancerous growth, and the facial palsy of a seventh cranial nerve lesion are all easily noted. And there's myxoedema, the condition caused by a paucity of thyroid hormone. The symptoms include obesity, dry hair and slowness of movement. A pathognomonic facial appearance is usually associated with the disease. And the lady flicking at the tablecloth had myxoedema. I was certain of that.

She'd finished and disappeared again, as mysteriously as

she'd arrived, when Dr Coleman arrived.

'Weak vegetable soup and lamb chops,' he said as he sat down opposite me.

'Have you seen the menu?' I asked innocently.

'It's Wednesday,' he said. 'It's always weak vegetable soup and lamb chops on Wednesday. And spotted dick,' he sighed.

'I hate weak vegetable soup, lamb chops and spotted dick.'

'Isn't there anything else?'

He shook his head. As he did so the myxoedematous waitress reappeared carrying two bowls of weak vegetable soup.

'I heard you come in, Doctor,' she said to my luncheon companion. 'I've brought your soup.'

'Thank you, Ethel.'

She shuffled off, the tea-towel tucked into her belt.

'Is her name really Ethel?' I whispered, leaning across the table.

'Her name's really Ruby, but everyone calls her Ethel.' I didn't like to ask why.

'Sad about that young patient of yours,' he went on, reaching out and taking a piece of bread from the raffiawork basket which stood beside the plated-silver cruet set.

'Miss Richards?'

'That's right,' he nodded, his mouth full of bread.

'Why?' I asked, with my first spoonful of soup in mid-air.

'She's got acute leukaemia,' he said, looking across at me. 'Didn't you know?'

Chapter Twenty One

During the next three days I spent a good deal of time with Ellen Richards. The laboratory tests had shown that she was suffering from a virulent and lethal form of leukaemia for which there was unlikely to be any cure. In blunter terms, she was dying.

No one had told her that, of course. Her general practitioner had merely suggested that a few hospital tests might be useful. Her consultant physician, Dr Younger, had explained to her that she had a blood deficiency that would make her feel rather weak; the medical registrar, Dr Sid, had spoken to her only twice, and then simply to ask for specific information about her medical history. As the acting house physician I was the representative of the medical profession officially responsible for her day-to-day care, and in consequence I had the job of answering her questions about her own condition. It was me she asked, 'When am I going to get better?'

'I'm not sure,' I lied. 'The tests haven't been completed yet.'

'They've been taking blood from me every day since I came into hospital,' she pointed out. 'Surely you must know something by now.'

I explained that the results were equivocal and that Dr Younger had not yet made a firm diagnosis.

'Is it serious?' she asked me. 'Tell me if it's serious.'

'Oh, I don't think so,' I told her with what I hoped was a smile. 'You'll be up and about soon.'

Then I made some excuse about having to go and see a patient on the male medical ward and rushed off, white coat billowing behind me importantly.

Instead, however, I went back to the doctors' residence. One of the house surgeons, whom I knew vaguely, was sitting in the dining-room eating pieces of dry bread and drinking cold coffee. He told me he'd missed breakfast.

'Do you always tell patients the truth?' I asked him suddenly.

'Pardon?'

I explained that I wanted advice.

'I never know,' he admitted. 'People are different.' He swallowed another mouthful of cold coffee and shuddered with distaste.

'But in general,' I insisted. 'What do you think in general terms?'

'Would you want to know if you were dying?' he asked me unexpectedly.

'I don't know. I've never thought about it.'

'Well, I've thought about it,' he told me, 'and I still don't know.' He put the last piece of bread into his mouth, pushed his chair back and stood up. 'Sorry,' he said, 'you'll just have to worry about it. Same as the rest of us.'

And worry I did. Ellen said she wanted to know the truth.

But did she really mean it? Could she be sure she wanted to know? Did I have the right or the courage to tell her? Had she guessed something? The questions were interminable and the answers equivocal.

She talked to me at length about herself and her family. Her father had built up a small chain of tobacconist shops, having started with a kiosk in a local hotel. Now he controlled seven shops and fifteen kiosks.

He was still proud of his humble origins and almost deliberately took pleasure in rejecting all his wife's attempts to tidy up his rough patches. Ellen's mother had taken their social rise far more seriously and she enjoyed being able to mix with the wives of executives and professional men.

Inevitably, therefore, they had numerous arguments, and frequently separated for days at a time. They always went back together in the end, however, being held in a tight marital bond by a desperate need for each other. At first, so she told me, Ellen had been deeply hurt when her parents quarrelled. Later she began to understand that the harsh words they threw at each other were intended not to hurt but to ease temporary pains. The reconciliations were always warm and full of genuine tenderness.

She talked to me about their love for her, their only child, which she knew was almost unlimited, and, as she described how each of them supported the other in times of crisis whatever the nature of any previous difference, it became clear to me that she knew she was dying. She was describing to me what she hoped would happen to her parents. For it was their sorrow which troubled her most.

Still I couldn't answer her questions with any honesty when they came. And they came daily; several times a day, in fact. Could I deprive her of whatever hopes she had? But how could I deny the inevitable, when she was so clearly becoming weaker hour by hour? Three days after I'd first met her she was so weak that she couldn't even sit up in bed without help.

'Tell me about yourself,' she said to me one day, after I'd sat listening to her for forty minutes. 'You know everything about me, but I know nothing at all about you.'

I replied that there was nothing much to tell.

'What sort of doctor are you going to be?' she insisted. 'You must tell me.'

I'd explained to her soon after my first examination of her that I was still a student.

I told her I didn't know.

'Are you going to specialise?' she asked. 'Or work in hospital?'

'Most specialists do work in hospital,' I told her.

'Do you want to work in hospital?'

'I don't know.'

'I think you ought to be a general practitioner.'

I asked her why.

'I don't know,' she said, putting her head on one side, and looking at me. 'I think you'd make a good general practitioner.' She smiled at me. 'You're too gentle to work in hospitals.'

I looked down at my hands and blushed.

'You know I'm dying, don't you?'

I said nothing.

'What have I got?' she asked me. 'What is it?'

I reached out for her hand and looked up at her. She looked straight at me, pleading for help, support, truth — I didn't know what. And then, suddenly, I told her. I told her that she had leukaemia, and that there was nothing anyone could do, and, as I told her, the tears streamed down my cheeks and I hated medicine, hated the Kintbury General Hospital, hated my own uselessness, hated everything. What was I doing? What were we all doing? Why did we have to let this girl die?

My maudlin self-pity and despair were suspended for a while when I was tapped on the shoulder by a staff nurse who told me that there was an emergency on the men's medical ward and they hadn't been able to get hold of either Dr Sid or Dr Coleman.

'I'll be back,' I promised Ellen, holding on to her fingers for a moment longer than might have been necessary. She smiled at me and nodded.

The emergency patient turned out to be a five-year-old boy who'd been admitted for some investigations. He'd broken his left leg twice, his right leg once, his right arm once and his left arm three times, and at last it had been decided that there might be some underlying bone pathology to account for these frequent fractures. The local children's hospital, which was supposed to cope with all patients under the age of twelve, had been shut down so that the decorators could paint over the cracks and mould which had decorated the wards for half a century, so all emergency admissions had to be brought into the Kintbury General. Michael Jones was the only child on the ward, and as a result the nurses had been spoiling him terribly.

'We let him sit out on the balcony,' explained the staff nurse breathlessly as we hurried towards the male ward. 'He was sitting there scribbling in a notebook we'd given him, when he was stung by a bee. He must be allergic to bees,' she went on. 'He's reacted very badly. He's all swollen up and Sister says she thinks he might die.'

I desperately tried to decide what I needed to do. I had great difficulty in dragging my mind back from Ellen Richards.

Bee, wasp and hornet stings usually produce nothing much more than a painful red swelling with some itching and some aching. However, on occasion, either because the victim has been stung before, because he's been stung by numerous bees, or because he has a natural allergy to bee stings, there may be a great danger of death. These minute arthropods are reported to cause more deaths in America each year than the much feared rattlesnakes.

Young Michael Jones was gasping for breath and restless and looked blue. He was more or less unconscious when I arrived by his bedside. As I sprinted down the ward towards him, completely ignoring the unwritten regulation that no one ever runs in a hospital, all I could think of was 'adrenalin'. That word kept leaping to the forefront of my mind.

'Adrenalin,' I shouted at the sister, who was trying to keep him from throwing himself off his bed.

The staff nurse who'd accompanied me grabbed an ampoule from the trolley that had already been wheeled into position, broke its top off, tore a syringe and then a needle out of their plastic packs, fitted the needle on to the syringe and drew up the contents of the ampoule. She handed the syringe to me. The ward sister held the boy's arm steady for me and, without bothering to hunt for cotton wool or methylated spirit, I jabbed the needle straight in and pressed the plunger. The syringe emptied rapidly; I stood back with it empty in my hand. I was trembling.

That was all I did. The sister and two nurses did all the rest, soothing, calming and restraining young Michael Jones. When Dr Sid and Dr Coleman arrived from the casualty department half an hour later, the patient was looking considerably better and I was feeling a great deal worse. It had been the first crisis I'd encountered on my own and, although the nurses had done much more than I had, there was no escaping the fact that young Michael could have died — but hadn't.

An hour later, sipping tea in the doctors' residence, I was still suffering from shock. I had to hold the cup with both hands to stop it spilling. I was rescued from this sad and depressing state by a telephone call from the hospital's administrative offices. They were worried because I'd somehow managed to arrive at the hospital without filling in the usual forms.

‘We haven’t any record of you,’ the clerk explained. ‘It’s most irregular.’

I apologised.

‘If you could come over now it would be a great help,’ she explained. ‘There’re a few things we need to get straightened out.’ She told me they needed to know where I’d be staying and how long I’d be there for. They also wanted to know if I had a national insurance card. I explained that I was already staying in the doctors’ residence, that I didn’t know how long I’d be there and that I didn’t have a national insurance card.

‘I’m afraid the hospital secretary still wants a word with you.’

Defeated, I made my way across to his office.

‘Thank you for coming,’ he said. ‘Just a few formalities.’

He smiled and bent forward a little. His eyes narrowed as he stared at my chin.

‘Right,’ I said.

‘Are you growing a beard?’ he asked me suddenly.

‘A beard?’ I repeated. I was still thinking about young Michael Jones.

‘Are you growing a beard? It’s against hospital regulations, you know.’

‘No, I’m not,’ I told him. I automatically reached up and felt my chin. ‘Oh, this,’ I said, understanding. ‘No. I forgot my razor and I haven’t had time to get one yet.’

The administrator said nothing. Then he swallowed and handed me two long forms to fill in. I scribbled my name on the bottoms and answered the questions that I could understand.

On my way out of his office, one of his receptionists stopped me. ‘Are you Dr Vernon?’

‘Edward Vernon,’ I replied carefully.

‘There’s a message for you from the female medical ward,’ she told me. ‘They thought you’d like to know that Miss Richards just died.’

Chapter Twenty Two

I needed to get away from the Kintbury General for a few hours. It's said that people get used to anything and that repeated exposure to difficult situations produces immunity. It wasn't working that way with me. For what seemed like a lifetime I'd been coming face to face with death, and still it was as hard as ever to accept. I continued to allow myself to become emotionally involved with patients, so that each loss still left me defeated and depressed. Living with pain and discomfort, fear and suffering, grief and bitterness is not easy. It's no wonder that medicine is riddled with remorse and recriminations and that the lawyers are beginning to move in and take over the profession. It's too easy for patients, doctors, relatives and nurses all to blame each other. In St Peter's there was some chance of escaping for a while into the more rarefied world of academic life, where reality is kept at bay by well-built barriers of intellectual pride. At the Kintbury General, where they dealt daily with an unending stream of sick and needy without enough equipment or staff, the pressure was remorseless. I could understand why Dr Younger felt so bitter. I had to get away for a while. I could hardly believe I'd been there for less than a week.

I needed to get back to the flat for another, more prosaic, reason. My beard was developing into a recognisable growth and despite my earlier denials I'd grown the outline of a full set of whiskers. I didn't like them, and I wanted to take them off. They made me look far more piratical than I felt.

Dr Sid and Dr Coleman cheerfully agreed to cover for me while I spent one night away. I couldn't ask Dr Younger's permission; he was at a conference in Bavaria where he was expected to stay for a week. The conference had been organised by the makers of Angipax, who had little difficulty in persuading several dozen British hospital consultants to abandon the tedium of day-to-day practical medicine for an opportunity to experience some genuine Teutonic hospitality. Attendance at two or three lectures and a certain moral commitment to prescribe Angipax was a small price to pay for such a trip, particularly since the visit was considered by the hospital to be educational and not vacational, so all expenses were paid.

Getting back into town was easier than getting out had been. Bus routes from the city centre spread outwards like the spokes of a wheel. It was easy to travel along the wrong one from the centre, but from the rim one had only to choose a bus travelling in the correct direction in order to find oneself in the centre. From the stop I walked to St Peter's and the flat.

Hector was sitting in the hall surrounded by pieces of machinery and wire. He looked as if he was about to start building a full-sized model of an Apollo spacecraft.

'It's a projector,' he explained. 'Bought it in a jumble sale for a couple of quid.'

'Does it work?'

'Not yet, but it will.'

'What on earth do you want a projector for anyway?'

I picked up a large, round, shiny can.

'Be careful with that!' said Hector rather sharply.

I put it down. 'What are you going to do with this?' I asked again.

'Show films. Good job you happened to call in — we're having a bit of a party tonight. You don't mind, do you?'

'Of course not.'

'You're invited, naturally.'

'Anything in particular that you're celebrating?' I asked him.

'It's a bit of a secret as a matter of fact,' he whispered confidentially, struggling for the fifth time to persuade a small length of spring to stay in position, 'but I don't mind telling you. I've been doing a bit of work with Mr Knibb, and it's been accepted for publication in the British Medical Journal.' He concentrated on fitting a screw into place.

'Congratulations,' I said, gathering that the news was worthy of them. 'Who is Mr Knibb?'

'He's one of the neurosurgeons. In fact, he's one of the leading neurosurgeons in the world.'

I hadn't heard of him, but I didn't like to admit it.

'He does some work at St Peter's, but a lot of his research is done in one of the Medical Research Council's laboratories in Cardiff. He's been kind enough to offer me his house job.'

'I thought you were going to study anaesthetics or radiology or something.'

'Ah, well,' said Hector with a slight smile. 'You know how it is. These opportunities come up and you can't afford to ignore them.' With a triumphant gesture he fitted the casing on to the projector and leant back admiringly.

'Who's coming to the party, then?'

'Two chaps from the neurosurgical unit and a few of the technicians. And a few nurses, of course.'

'Should be a good crowd.'

He was lifting up the projector to stand it on a small table that usually carried a bowl of hideous artificial flowers made of luminous red and green plastic, when Andrew and Sara appeared. It was good to see them both. I shook hands with Andrew and kissed Sara on the cheek. 'D'you like it, then?' Andrew asked.

I looked at him, rather puzzled.

'What d'you think of it?' he demanded. He put his arm round Sara and smiled down at her. She smiled back at him, and I felt distinctly superfluous. 'The jumper,' he explained, pulling at a patterned sweater he was wearing. 'Sara knitted it for me.'

I made polite, congratulatory noises which probably sounded trite, but were genuine, and Sara looked suitably embarrassed. Andrew just looked extraordinarily proud both of his sweater and his girlfriend.

'You off out?' Hector asked him, adjusting the legs of the projector so that it was level. The table had one leg shorter than the other three.

'I'm taking Sara into town. She's got to meet her parents. They're taking her out for a meal.' I gathered that Andrew wasn't included in the invitation. I told Sara that I hoped we'd meet again soon, and promised Andrew that I'd see him at the party.

When they'd gone I watched Hector threading the film

through.

'I got this one from a lab technician in the pathology department,' he explained. 'It's rather good. Do you want to have a preview with me?'

I told him that I had a few things to do at the hospital and that I'd see him later. In fact, I'd intended to go along to the medical school library and get some bookwork done but I stopped off in the cafeteria and drank two cups of steaming hot coffee with a couple of fellows who were in the same year as Hector, Andrew and I but whom I'd hardly seen for more than six months. That's one of the funny things about studying medicine: everyone moves around from hospital to hospital and department to department, and the people you're supposed to be studying with are almost total strangers by the time you qualify.

* * *

It was eight when I got back to the flat, and the party had already started; surprisingly early, for most medical students' parties started nearer the day on which they would finish. I was astonished to find that most of the people there were dressed in dinner jackets or long dresses; and even more surprised to see that the men were wearing the dinner jackets and the women the dresses.

'I'm sorry,' I apologised to Hector. 'I haven't got a dinner jacket.'

'That's fine,' he reassured me. 'Just put a tie on, will you? It's supposed to be sort of semi-formal.'

I brushed some of the creases out of my cleanest white shirt and gave my sports jacket a bit of a shake. I even polished the leather elbow-patches.

Hector had fitted up the projector so that it was aimed at a good-sized expanse of flat wall; he was carefully threading the film into position. He didn't seem anxious to begin a conversation, so I wandered slowly into the bathroom where the drinks had been laid out on two old planks resting across the bath. A tall, rather elegant man with a droopy carnation pinned to his dinner jacket was busy pouring generous measures of home-made wine into long-stemmed glasses. Hector must have hired those — our guests normally drank from a motley collection of half-pint beer-glasses, coffee-cups, mugs and free gifts which had been handed out to previous occupants of the flat mobile enough to patronise petrol stations. The elegant guest's friend, a willowy creature with no back to her dress and not much front to her body, was chattering prettily about someone called Rita.

'I think it's awful the way she's always gossiping about people,' she complained. 'I hate gossip; it's so demeaning.'

'Absolutely, dear,' said the elegant man, picking up four glasses in one hand and taking her arm with the other. He led her past me, and out of the bathroom. Left alone, I poured a large quantity of the wine into the tooth-mug from the shelf over the washbasin, which held approximately twice as much fluid as the handsome long-stemmed glasses. Then I drifted back into the hall. By this time there were about twenty-five guests crowded into the flat — most of them squashed behind Hector and the projector. I half recognised two or three, but realised to my astonishment that most were total strangers. I'd heard that Hector's engagement had been broken off and the dietician's absence seemed to confirm the rumour.

With a few words of warning Hector reached up and switched off the hall-light. The projector began to purr and the film to whirr. The audience settled with some shuffling into the most comfortable positions they could find. I was standing in front of the projector but could just keep out of the spotlight by pressing back into my bedroom doorway.

The film was of the hue normally described as blue. An assortment of naked actresses and actors cavorted merrily from scene to scene using neither clothes nor plot to cloak their indecent activities. From the squeals and screams of delight coming from behind Hector, I could guess that the film was encouraging active participation among the audience. Perhaps I wasn't in the right mood for it; perhaps I'd have been more enthusiastic had I been accompanied by an imaginative partner. Anyway, my major reaction was one of astonishment that people who spent their daily lives in contact with naked people should be prepared to sit in desperately uncomfortable positions watching more naked people getting into desperately uncomfortable positions on a makeshift screen. I found myself watching the audience more than the entertainment.

When the film had been played through twice Hector turned it round and showed it backwards. That brought even louder screams of delight, as the protagonists extricated themselves with great speed and ease from their unusual positions. Then he showed it upside down. After that he turned the projector off and the lights on, and everyone queued for the bathroom; sixteen people wanted to get drinks, seven wanted to use the lavatory and one wanted to be sick. I know, because I was stuck in my bedroom doorway and I had to stand and watch them all.

When I finally managed to get into the bathroom myself I found Andrew sitting on the edge of the bath. He looked very miserable.

'Where've you been?' I asked him.

'In here,' he said flatly. He looked at his watch. 'I'm meeting Sara at the bus stop at eleven.'

'It's not ten yet,' I pointed out.

'I'm not much interested in the crowd Hector's invited.'

'You're just moping because Sara's off for the evening,' I told him. 'Anyone would think she'd gone out with someone else!'

'I think I'll go and wait at the bus stop,' he said gruffly. He seemed rather lost without Sara, and in a strange way I envied him.

* * *

Half an hour or so later Hector turned the projector round, opened the window at the far end of the hall and aimed the lens through it. The beam of light landed on an expensive house across the road where, judging by the cars in the drive, the guests were unlikely ever to be eligible for supplementary benefits.

A few moments later there were great squeals of delight as the front of the house was decorated with moving pictures of an unbelievably well-endowed young lady. Undoubtedly intrigued by the flood of light unexpectedly pouring into their living-room, the occupants and their guests began to trickle out through the front door. With surprising skill Hector managed to stop the projector so that the doorway was neatly positioned between the legs of the film's major star; the expensively dressed and expensively coiffured men and women who wandered, blinking, out into the evening light appeared to be making their exits from the film star's perineal portals. No one except me seemed to notice that the third person to appear on the doorstep was Professor Grainger.

It was he who knocked on the door of the flat a few seconds later.

I expected the worst, but he stayed for nearly an hour, aiming the projector in turn at his fellow-guests across the road and directing different mammoth organs on to their grinning faces. When he left he clapped Hector on the shoulder and congratulated him on his imagination. I was so relieved that I drank far too much home-made wine.

When I caught the bus back to the Kintbury General at seven the following morning I forgot my razor again.

Chapter Twenty Three

The bus driver inched his way through the traffic. He stopped for every car, lorry, pedestrian, cyclist and small animal anxious to cross our path or join the flow of traffic. When I got back to the Kintbury General, Ethel, the white-coated, myxoedematous dining-room assistant, was clearing the table. Reluctantly she left two slices of toast, and the half-cupful of coffee that remained in a chipped white porcelain jug. I gulped down the coffee and swallowed the toast without even taking the time to smear it with marmalade.

Dr Sid and Dr Coleman were already on the male medical ward. A twenty-year-old Italian with meningitis was struggling and shouting as they attempted to perform a lumbar puncture. There didn't seem anything I could do to help and, with two porters and three nurses also crowded into the confined area around his bed, there was no room for spectators. The porters were there to keep the patient still, the nurses to keep Dr Sid and Dr Coleman supplied with sterile quantities of all the necessary bits and pieces of equipment. I walked back along the ward and stopped by Mr Kennedy's bed. A young student nurse was washing him.

Someone had provided him with a proper black eye-patch and he looked truly piratical. A small pile of magazines on his bedside table made it clear that he'd continued to improve his reading.

'He's doing very well, aren't you, Pop?' said the student nurse.

Mr Kennedy slowly nodded and smiled slightly. I felt that she was detracting from his dignity by using such a general endearment, but I didn't say anything. Draping a small towel across his middle she washed with a soapy yellow sponge as far down as possible, then as far up as possible.

'Sister said he can go outside in a wheelchair if it's sunny,' she said.

'Great,' I agreed. She wiped the remains of the soap from her patient and rubbed him dry with a thick white towel. When she'd finished, he reached out and touched her hand for a moment.

She helped him back into his pyjamas and combed his hair.

He'd already been shaved. 'There you are, Pop,' she said finally. She could hardly have been more than eighteen, and she was bathing a man old enough to be her grandfather. Hardly surprising, perhaps, that to protect her own sanity she had to remove in her mind his personal identity and natural human independence.

'I'll help you into a wheelchair,' I told him. I asked the nurse to wait while I fetched one from the corridor. There were nearly always a couple stored there, just as at St Peter's. I was beginning to learn that, despite the obvious, major differences between them, all hospitals follow certain patterns of organisation simply because, although they may be arbitrary, they're also efficient.

The two of us helped him into the chair, pulling his old checked woollen dressing-gown around him while he was standing up. I put a couple of magazines in his lap, added the newspaper and a bag of peppermints he pointed to, and proceeded to push him out of the ward, out of the hospital and into the grounds.

The sun was warm enough to be pleasant but not hot enough to be stifling. I found him a sheltered corner near the goldfish pond and hurried back to the ward. On the way I passed young Michael Jones, now clearly recovered from his bee sting. He, too, was in pyjamas and dressing-gown.

'Does the sister know you're down here?' I asked him.

He nodded. 'She said it was all right as long as I didn't go too far.'

'Well, you mind you don't.' He scampered off before I'd said it, waving goodbye.

Mr Kennedy's improvement had cheered me considerably. He still couldn't speak, and his movements were weak and often imprecise, but he could do a great deal more for himself than when I'd first seen him on my first day at the Kintbury General. For months after a stroke, patients often make tremendous strides, recovering many of the abilities they and their relatives and healers often feel are lost forever. With a little luck and a great deal of perseverance Mr Kennedy might well recover his speech and learn to walk again. The speech therapist and physiotherapists would continue to work away with him, and as long as he continued to improve he would be encouraged. The main danger was that he'd abandon hope, and then find himself simply a burden on an acute medical ward where beds are always at a premium. Then he might well be transferred to a geriatric hospital from where there would be no escape. He'd almost certainly never be able to live alone at home — even when I'd first met him he'd been too badly affected by the narrowing of the arteries supplying his brain for that — but he could possibly manage to live with some assistance in a sheltered flat or an old people's residential home where the occupants are allowed freedom to look after their own spirits, if not their bodies. The progress he made in the next few weeks would determine precisely what was to happen to him.

I pondered on his prospects while I admitted an elderly woman to the ward for tests on her thyroid gland and took blood samples from the dozen or so patients on both the male and female wards who needed investigations. While I'd been at the Kintbury General I'd acquired several new technical skills, and I'd greatly improved my ability to remove blood without alienating the patient. Practice makes perfect, they say.

'Can you take some blood from Michael Jones?' asked Dr Coleman, who'd finished treating the Italian with meningitis and was heading back to the doctors' residence to change his clothes. He'd managed to get his trousers covered not with spinal fluid, blood or drip-solution but with lemon squash. The almost obligatory bottle of squash on the bedside table had been sent flying by one of the porters as they'd struggled to keep the patient still enough.

I promised to find young master Michael and do my best.

Children's veins are inevitably smaller than those of adults, and extracting blood from a child is often a difficult and tiresome business. Michael wasn't on the ward, so I stuffed into my coat pocket the necessary syringe, needle, sample-bottle and swab. Then I headed for where I'd last seen him.

For ten minutes I scoured the grounds until I eventually arrived where I'd left Mr Kennedy. When I saw the wheelchair I hurried forward; my patient was lying prone on the ground, stretched forward in front of it.

I expected to find him dead or dying, but he wasn't. His eyes, however, were full of terror. He looked at me in absolute agony and slowly managed to lift his right arm to point towards the goldfish pond.

'What is it?' I asked him. Stooping down to attend to him, I looked behind me to see what he was pointing at. I could spot nothing of any significance.

Eyes wide with desperation, he tried to edge himself forward along the gravel path. He managed only an inch or two. Clearly, for some reason, he'd been deliberately moving from his wheelchair towards the pond. I stood up and walked quickly in the direction he was pointing.

I was about a yard and a half from the pond when I saw why Mr Kennedy was so desperate. At the same time I saw why I'd been unable to find Michael Jones. He was lying face down in the pond, his dressing-gown billowing around him. He must have fallen in while kneeling or standing on the edge. He'd probably been trying to touch one of the goldfish.

I turned back to Mr Kennedy. He must have watched it all from his wheelchair, unable to move, unable to shout for help. Gently I lifted Michael out of the water and laid him down beside the pool; then I helped Mr Kennedy back into his wheelchair. His eyes were shut and he sobbed continuously.

Two porters carefully carried Michael to the pathology examination room. He'd been dead for some time and there was no chance of resuscitating him. I wheeled Mr Kennedy back on to the ward and, with the help of the student nurse who'd helped me before, I got him back into bed. He seemed weaker and more frail than he had only a couple of hours ago.

Chapter Twenty Four

It was my first night on call by myself. I was sole representative of the medical profession in a hospital whose two medical wards contained forty-seven patients and whose casualty department catered for a total population of over one hundred and fifty thousand. There was a house surgeon on call, but his responsibilities were confined to the two surgical wards; there was a doctor whose job was to look after the pregnant women and those with gynaecological disorders. But for purely medical problems I was the physician at whose feet the buck paused, even if it didn't actually stop for good.

Beside my bed I'd put three books on medical emergencies which I'd taken out of the hospital's small library. I'd carefully marked the pages dealing with specific problems so that without delay I could refresh my memory of how best to deal with a coronary, a pneumothorax, a bleeding duodenal ulcer an attack of status epilepticus, cirrhosis, acute pancreatitis, a diabetic coma, pneumonia, a stroke, meningitis, malaria, relapsing fever, ooncherciasis, food poisoning, typhoid fever, von Recklinghausen's disease or an asthmatic attack.

At half-past eleven, having already dealt with several small medical problems, I lay down on top of the bed. I didn't bother to remove my white coat or even my shoes. I knew that somehow this time was different, and I wouldn't sleep. Always before there had been someone else around. Now there wasn't; Dr Coleman was enjoying a night at the cinema with a staff nurse and unlikely to return until breakfast-time.

Dr Sid, also off duty, had travelled up to Manchester for the night to visit friends and attend a birthday party. Officially he was always on call and I could, if I needed help, reach him at his hotel. He'd given me the number. That was, however, of limited value. There wasn't much of a chance that he could ever get back from Manchester in time to do more than sign the death certificate.

I fully intended to stay awake all night, ready to fly off at an instant's notice to provide succour and professional help to anyone in need. Nevertheless, despite all my good intentions, I was asleep when the phone finally did ring. It woke me with a start, for I still hadn't developed that strange facility for coming out of a deep sleep within seconds, nor acquired the doctor's habit of cat-napping through the night, ready to be awakened by the slightest hint of a bell. Now, when I'm on call at night, a typewriter bell can wake me at a hundred yards. Then it was different; when I fell asleep, I fell asleep.

'Right,' I stuttered into the telephone, throwing myself out of bed and fumbling underneath it for my shoes.

The caller told me there was a problem on the female medical ward. Tearing off my white coat and tie, I promised to be there straight away. Only when I'd put the phone down did I realise that I'd deliberately remained dressed and that my shoes were on my feet. And it wasn't until I was half way through the door that I realised I'd forgotten to ask what the trouble was. My carefully prepared index of emergency treatments was quite useless without a diagnosis to work on.

The patient was a forty-three-year-old woman with a long history of asthmatic attacks. She'd been admitted by Dr Coleman when I'd been at Hector's party.

'She's gradually been getting worse for the last hour or so,' said the nurse on duty — the same student who'd helped me with Mr Kennedy. Now she was in charge of a ward full of acute medical cases. She seemed to be alone.

Mrs Hinton was clearly having difficulty in getting her breath. I listened to her chest and heard nothing much except the strained wheezing so typical of the true asthmatic.

'Could you get me some aminophylline, please?' I asked the nurse, in a whisper. The ward was in darkness except for Mrs Hinton's bedside lamp and a dim light on the nurse's desk. Several of the patients were snoring heavily, and one was talking in her sleep. She seemed to be having an argument with her husband or boyfriend.

The nurse tiptoed down the ward to the sister's office and the drug cupboard. Then she tiptoed back again.

'It's locked,' she told me.

'Haven't you got the key?'

She shook her head. 'I'm not qualified. I'm not allowed it.' It was only then that I realised that the whole ward, Mrs Hinton included, was at the mercy of two unqualified people. It was perhaps a good job that most of them were sleeping soundly.

I found a steel ruler on the sister's desk and managed to break the cupboard open. I found an ampoule of aminophylline and injected it into Mrs Hinton. Immediately she began to breathe more easily.

'When are you off duty?' I asked the nurse when we'd cleared away the debris and turned off Mrs Hinton's lamp. We were standing in darkness in the sister's office.

She told me she would finish her night-duty rota two days later.

'Will you come out with me?' I asked her. 'We could have a meal somewhere.'

No sooner had she said she would than the night's stillness and the romantic mood were broken by the heavy click-clack of a pair of approaching feet. The nurse, whose name I still didn't know, leapt away from me.

'Everything all in order?' asked the night sister sharply.

'What's been going on here?'

'I came up to see Mrs Hinton,' I explained. I was automatically on the defensive. It seemed as if the sister suspected that my visit to the ward wasn't entirely on clinical grounds.

'Hmph,' she snorted. She brushed past us both and on into the office. It was then she saw the cupboard.

'What's happened?' she asked, panicking. 'Someone's been in the drug cupboard. Call the police at once!' She reached over for the telephone. I put my hand on top of hers to stop her making the call.

'It's all right,' I explained. 'I had to open it to get some aminophylline out.'

She looked at me in horror. 'You broke into the drug cupboard?'

I nodded.

'Aren't you the student?'

I nodded again.

'But you're not allowed into the drug cupboard.' She sat down. This is very serious.'

I pointed out that Mrs Hinton had been ill and was now better. I also explained that although neither of us was qualified we were the only people available at that moment.

'You could have called me,' said the sister indignantly.

'The switchboard always knows where I am. Anyway, I've got a bleep.'

I pointed out that legally, even if we called her, we still couldn't do anything with the aminophylline unless we either found Dr Coleman or brought Dr Sid back from Manchester. At that point she rather haughtily told the pair of us that she'd have to report the whole incident to the matron and Dr Younger and that someone would have to pay for the cupboard to be repaired. Then she went. We didn't hear any more about it, and the cupboard remained unlockable until the day I left Kintbury General.

***

Having a date with a nurse to keep me awake I went back to bed. Twice more that night I was called to the casualty department, once to suture a small cut caused in a fist-fight and once to check a patient who'd fallen off his bicycle. He seemed to have survived. After that I fell soundly asleep until the telephone rang for a fourth time at half-past six. This time it was the student nurse on the male medical ward. It seemed the whole hospital was being managed by unqualified staff.

'Can't it wait until the morning ward-round?' I begged sleepily. The night had been long and I hadn't slept anywhere near enough. Not only had I worked all the previous day but I would, of course, be working all the following day.

'I'm sorry to bother you, but I'm very worried,' she said unhappily.

'What's the trouble?' I asked, still trying to get out of the call.

'I don't know,' she said with a trace of fear in her voice.

'I think someone's dying.'

'OK,' I sighed. 'I'll come up.' I clambered off the bed again and stumbled sleepily towards the door. For the fourth time I'd forgotten to get any information, and my filing system of treatments was still lying useless on the floor. I made a mental note to write out some small crib-cards to carry with me so that I could take the essence of my library in my pocket. I was fairly confident I could make the necessary diagnosis but nowhere near so sure of deciding on the right treatment.

As I made my way from the doctors' residence to the hospital I couldn't help cursing quietly. I wasn't cursing anything in particular but I found myself looking forward to the time when I could just lie down and sleep. People who kept waking me up were not high on my list of friends.

'It's the gentleman down there,' said the nurse when I arrived, 'but I think he's dead.' She bit her lower lip and bravely fought back the tears. 'I've never had a patient die before.'

The patient was dead. It was Mr Kennedy, and he'd had another stroke; this time one large enough to kill him. I closed his eyes with my thumbs and put his black eye-patch in my pocket while the nurse adjusted the sheets. Ever since young Michael Jones had drowned, Mr Kennedy had slipped backwards, resisting all attempts by the physiotherapists or the speech therapist to help him improve his strength. It was as though he'd decided to die.

Wearily I stumbled back to my bedroom. Somehow it hadn't really sunk in and it didn't really matter very much. I was so tired that I was almost relieved I didn't have to do anything but go back and sleep. Sleep, that is, if the telephone didn't ring.

Chapter Twenty Five

The phone didn't ring again, and I woke to find the house-keeper shaking my shoulder and waving a cup of hot, sweet tea under my nose. Wearily I lurched out of bed ready for another day. Since I still had no razor, my early-morning chores were reduced to the basic minimum, and five or six minutes later I was struggling into my white coat. It was only when I put my hand into the pocket and discovered Mr Kennedy's eye-patch that I remembered what had happened the night before.

Depressed again, I sat down at breakfast to find a brown envelope on my plate. Inside was a letter from the hospital secretary telling me that a new house physician was due to start that day. Since I'd no longer be required as a locum I was free to return to St Peter's.

I read it with mixed feelings. Mr Kennedy's death following so quickly after the deaths of Michael Jones and Ellen Richards had left me emotionally exhausted. I'd be pleased to get back to the comparative peace and quiet of the teaching hospital. Besides, I had a great deal of bookwork to do, and at the Kintbury General I didn't have much time for reading. There were final examinations to be taken before too long, and a lot to be learnt in a rapidly shrinking amount of time.

On the other hand, I'd be sad to leave the hospital where I had in a sense come of age and where I'd learnt something of the true nature of medical practice. In retrospect the five years of my medical education are something of a blur. Like any autobiographer, I've had to concentrate on the events which stand out.

But there were plenty of those at the Kintbury General. When I arrived I'd been very unsure of myself and completely without confidence. When I left I still recognised that I had much to learn, but because I'd been promoted into a situation of responsibility I'd had to acquire confidence quickly. And I'd made good friends there, too. Dr Sid, whose quiet and efficient way of working hardly attracted anyone's attention, had a cool, clinical approach to every problem. Watching him taught me the value of that. And Dr Coleman, more flamboyant and more likely to become emotionally involved with the patients in his care, had his faults and virtues, too.

I told Dr Coleman that I was leaving. He wished me well and said he hoped that the new house physician did at least speak some English. He said he'd got used to being able to talk to his colleague.

The many-chinned waitress dropped a plateful of eggs and bacon in front of me and shuffled away.

'Hasn't she got myxoedema?' I asked Dr Coleman.

He shook his head. 'Ethel,' he called, ignoring my protests.

She turned round and came back towards the table.

'Ethel,' he said, 'take your hat off.'

She grinned toothlessly at him, reached up and whipped off her hair. Underneath it she was completely bald.

'Everyone thinks she's got myxoedema,' he assured me, 'but she lost her hair in the war when her house was bombed.' She grinned at me and put it back on. Now I'd seen her without it, I recognised it as a pretty cheap and poor imitation of a head of hair. That did explain, however, why it had seemed to me to have the dry quality of myxoedematous hair.

After I'd finished breakfast I went on to the wards to say goodbye to the nurses and patients. The student with whom I'd made a date was just leaving the female medical ward.

'You're late off duty,' I exclaimed, looking at my watch.

'There's been a bit of a fuss.'

'Not over the drug cupboard?'

'No,' she said, 'but we forgot to write up the aminophylline in Mrs Hinton's records and on her drug chart.'

I apologised, since that was mainly my fault. The nurse had obviously been crying.

'They didn't tell you off too much, did they?' I asked her.

She shook her head. 'I couldn't care less about that,' she told me. 'I think I'm giving up nursing anyway.'

'Why?' I asked, astonished.

'I've just heard about Mr Kennedy,' she said. 'He was a lovely old man, wasn't he?'

I agreed that he was.

'I'm going home to Shrewsbury when my night duty's finished,' she told me. 'I'm glad I saw you now.'

'Oh' was all I could say. I didn't tell her that I wouldn't be around the Kintbury General much longer, either.

'I'm sorry about the date. But thank you for asking me.'

'That's the story of my life,' I shrugged, resorting to the old cliché in lieu of anything more sensible.

Then she disappeared, off to bed, and I went on to the ward. Mrs Hinton was sitting in a chair reading the morning paper.

'Good morning, Dr Vernon,' she said cheerily. 'Thank you for coming last night.'

'I'm glad you're looking better.'

'Have a sweet,' she said, handing me a bag of acid drops.

Out of politeness I took one. She smiled at me gratefully.

Life in medicine wasn't all dismalness and despair. There were good moments which made it worthwhile. I took the morning blood samples then made my way back to pack my small bag. At the flat I would at least be able to have a shave. I was beginning to take on a distinctly nautical look.

Chapter Twenty Six

After the hectic technicolour world of the Kintbury General, life at St Peter's seemed positively monochromatic. The teaching hospital offered more exotic and unusual illnesses, but patients were diagnosed and treated at a rather more leisurely pace; in addition, I'd been in a position of responsibility at the Kintbury General. For a short time I'd worked as a doctor and been accepted as such by patients and staff alike; now I was simply a medical student again.

Andrew was in the kitchen when I'd finished shaving, and he called me as I came out of the bathroom.

'Great news,' he beamed. 'Sara and I are going to get married.'

'That's fantastic! When?'

'Haven't quite decided yet, but we'd like you to be the best man.'

I told him that I'd be honoured. We shook hands.

'We must have a drink,' I said. I began to rummage around in the kitchen cupboards. We kept a fairly catholic collection of items there: rubber gloves for when the sink became blocked up, old beer-bottles waiting to be returned to the off-licence, candles for use in the frequent power-cuts, and so on. But there was little food apart from a couple of pounds of potatoes which had sprouted. And no alcohol at all. Even the fridge was bare.

'I know,' I said suddenly. 'There's probably something left over from Hector's party. There were gallons of stuff.'

I sorted through the piles of sheets and old bottles in the airing cupboard, where I knew Hector kept his home-made wine. Andrew had followed me out from the kitchen.

'Here it is!' I said, eventually finding half a bottleful. 'I think his dad makes the stuff.'

'It doesn't look too good,' said Andrew suspiciously. 'When was it opened? Are you sure it's safe?'

'Well, Hector drinks a fair bit of it,' I laughed. 'Let's drink to you and Sara.' I didn't tell him I could see a dead spider floating on the surface. I thought it might put him off.

We found two coffee-mugs and emptied the bottle.

‘Funny stuff,’ said Andrew, wrinkling up his nose, ‘very odd.’

‘Grown on the shady side of the garage and the farthest corner of the airing cupboard.’

‘I’ve applied for a house job up north,’ he said, taking a cautious sip. ‘My relatives are up there and we’ll be glad to get away from Sara’s relatives. They haven’t taken to the wedding too well.’

‘Why not?’

‘Oh, they think I’m a bit of an oddball, I suppose.’ He took a second, less cautious sip. ‘And they think Sara’s still just looking for sympathy.’

‘When are you getting married? Before or after finals?’

‘Oh, after.’ He grinned. ‘You never know...!’

‘You won’t fail,’ I told him. ‘You’ve done too well to fail now.’

‘Oh, I don’t know,’ he sighed. ‘Professor Grainger still doesn’t like me too much, you know. They haven’t forgiven me for that piece I wrote.’ He finished off his wine.

‘Anyway,’ he said, suddenly changing his voice and the subject, ‘what are you planning to do?’

‘Haven’t got the foggiest idea,’ I confessed honestly.

‘Where are you doing your house jobs?’

‘I don’t know. I haven’t applied anywhere yet.’

‘You’ll have to get a move on, you know; the best jobs all go months in advance.’

‘I know,’ I nodded. ‘I just can’t make my mind up, though.’

‘Thought about what you’re going to do when the house jobs are over?’

I told him that I’d thought about it but hadn’t come to any conclusions. ‘I just don’t know what I want to do. I sometimes wonder about general practice, but I’m not sure whether I’d like it.’

‘They ought to let us have a look at a bit of general practice,’ argued Andrew, picking up my cup and finishing my wine. ‘You didn’t want this, did you?’

I shook my head.

‘I think I’ll go into general practice as soon as I’ve done

my house jobs. I might do a few months in obstetrics, but then I'll get a nice job as an assistant or a junior partner somewhere and settle down with Sara.'

'Where is she today?' I asked him, suddenly remembering that she'd been living with Andrew in the flat for some time.

'Her folks have sent her to spend a month with her granny in Canada. She didn't want to go but they pushed her into it.'

'Canada!'

'Her mother's Canadian. They told her it'd do her good to have a rest away from everything for a week or two.' He smiled ruefully. 'I rather got the impression that by "everything" they meant me,' he said.

'Have you met her dad?'

'Once.' Andrew looked extremely sleepy and I began to suspect that Hector's home-made wine might have matured into something a little more powerful. 'He's a funny bugger. Very cautious and careful. The sort of bloke who wears overshoes on top of his wellington boots.' He yawned.

'Perhaps when Sara comes back from Canada and they can see you're both still set on getting married, he'll come round to your point of view.'

'Maybe,' nodded Andrew. 'Maybe and maybe not.' He suddenly leant forward, put his head on the table and began to snore very loudly.

Leaving him fast asleep, I walked through pouring rain over to St Peter's. I'd been allocated to work for a week on the dermatological ward. Despite the fact that a great many patients visit their general practitioners with skin problems, dermatology isn't one of the areas of medicine taken most seriously by teaching-hospital mandarins. It's kept neatly in a niche with tropical diseases, dentistry, audiology and venereal disease. In seven days I'd be expected to learn all I needed to know about skin disorders.

My first patient was a middle-aged man who'd been admitted because of an irritating rash that had resisted all attempts at treatment. Even the universally useful steroid creams had proved ineffective, and Mr Kendall had been admitted to St Peter's so that the consultant dermatologist, Dr Meredith Morgan, could experiment with more powerful creams and ointments.

However, twelve hours after his admission and half an hour before I arrived at his bedside to examine him, Mr Kendall's rash had suddenly, inexplicably and totally disappeared.

'It's gone, Doctor,' he said happily. 'Gone completely. I'm very pleased.'

'But you haven't had any treatment yet, have you?'

He shook his head. 'The nurse said that Dr Morgan would be quite upset about it,' he frowned. 'I do hope he isn't too cross with me.'

'I'm sure he won't be,' I told him, although I was by no means certain. Dr Morgan had quite a reputation for being outspoken and sharp with his patients. He wouldn't like any of them to enjoy a miracle cure.

'While I'm here, though, Doctor,' said Mr Kendall cautiously and rather shyly, 'there is one other thing you might be able to help me with.'

'What's that?'

'I've got this lump.'

'Where?'

'Down near my privates,' he blushed. 'You know, my frilly bits.'

'Right,' I said. 'Let's have a look, then.'

I drew the screens around his bed and pulled the bed-clothes back. He unfastened and pulled down his pyjama trousers, revealing in his right groin the largest and most impressive-looking hernia I'd ever seen.

'There it is,' he said proudly. 'What d'you think of it?'

'Tremendous,' I said admiringly. 'Dr Morgan may be disappointed by the disappearance of your rash but Mr Meridew will be pleased with that.'

'Mr Meridew? Who's that?'

'He's a surgeon,' I explained. Gingerly I reached forward and touched the hernia. It was about the size of a decent-sized melon, and almost purple. I touched it gently and with the respect due a work of art.

'Does it go down at all?' I asked, removing my hand.

Mr Kendall shook his head.

'Never?'

'It used to — at least, it used to get a bit smaller occasionally. But it's been like that for ages now.'

I reached out again. It was quite hard and smooth. Then, as I allowed my fingers to rest on it, I noticed that it was beating away as though it contained a heart of its own. As cautiously as if it had been an explosive device I withdrew my hand. This was no ordinary hernia. In fact, it was no hernia at all. Mr Kendall, I suddenly realised, had a massive aneurysm in his groin.

An aneurysm forms when an artery dilates and a small blood-filled swelling appears. One of the big dangers with an aneurysm is that it can burst. The wall of the artery has been spread thinly and may explode at almost any time. With the blood inside under considerable pressure, a leaking aneurysm can quickly prove fatal.

Leaving Mr Kendall lying naked on top of his bed, since I didn't dare put the bedclothes back, I hurried to the nearest telephone and called Dr Morgan, who wasn't important enough to have a registrar of his own and whose resident houseman was on holiday. Dr Morgan was having dinner with a party of guests and his wife quizzed me for several minutes before reluctantly agreeing to fetch him from his meal. Dermatologists do not often have emergencies to cope with. While I waited I told the ward sister, who was looking at me with some astonishment, to prepare herself for a major emergency.

'Mr Kendall has an aneurysm,' I gasped when Dr Morgan had finally come on the line and I'd introduced myself.

'Has he?' he said, noisily chewing his supper.

'What shall we do?'

'What sort of aneurysm is it?'

'An enormous one.'

'Ah,' he said, rather drily. 'How long has he had it?'

I had to admit that I didn't know, so I asked him to wait while I rushed back and asked Mr Kendall how long the lump had been there.

‘Twenty-three years,’ I answered rather shamefully a few moments later.

‘Do you think it might hang on for another few hours?’ asked Dr Morgan.

I agreed that it might.

‘Perhaps until tomorrow morning?’ I said it seemed quite likely.

‘Then we’ll leave it alone for now,’ he said. ‘Good night.’ I said good night, too, and went and told Mr Kendall that he could put his pyjamas back on. As I left the ward the sister looked at me with a raised eyebrow.

‘Is the emergency over?’ she enquired with deliberate politeness.

Chapter Twenty Seven

There are several ways of annoying a ward sister. One of the most reliable is to sit on a patient's bed, rumpling the neatly folded, creaseless sheets and leaving behind a clear impression of the encounter. Ward sisters have a natural aversion to clutter, disorder and untidiness of any sort and are likely to turn very nasty when confronted with anyone less than a consultant sitting on an occupied bed.

'Would you like a chair, Mr Vernon?' enquired Sister Yardley coldly as I perched on the edge of Mr Kendall's bed in the intensive care unit. He'd been referred by Dr Morgan to Mr Meridew, who'd been quite enthralled by the prospect of exploring his groin. The swelling, it was universally agreed, was indeed an aneurysm, and Mr Meridew had cancelled two gall-bladder removals and a circumcision in order to make room for Mr Kendall in the theatre. He was anxious to operate quickly, not because he feared for Mr Kendall's life, but because he knew that the hospital's specialist cardiovascular surgeon, Mr Johnson, was due back from a conference in South Africa within the week. With Mr Johnson available, Mr Meridew would have no chance of getting his knife anywhere near an aneurysm. So Mr Kendall had been operated on with the minimum of delay and was now convalescing in the intensive care unit, a specially equipped small ward where eight highly qualified nurses and four even more highly qualified sisters looked after four patients at a time, on a rota system.

'I beg your pardon?' I enquired, half-moving off the bed.

'Would you like a chair?' repeated Sister Yardley, with rather more steel in her voice.

'That's very kind of you, Sister.'

'There's one over there.' She nodded towards the far corner of the unit where two stacking chairs were stored. She stood and watched, hands on her hips, as I fetched myself one and sat down on it. Then she turned round and without another word marched back into a glass-fronted office, where she could keep an eye on all her patients and on a bank of television screens and electrical dials which kept her up-to-date with their physiological status. As the senior nursing officer in charge of the intensive care unit she was on permanent day duty, while her husband, a charge nurse working in the Gregory Geriatric Hospital, worked on permanent nights. It was hardly surprising therefore that she sometimes snapped at medical students, visitors and junior doctors. The couple came together once a month or so when their off-duty coincided, and for two or three days after each connubial weekend she would smile sweetly at everyone and ignore all potential disasters with the cheerful disposition of a woman fresh from a romantic assignation.

'Nice to see you, Doctor,' said Mr Kendall.

'How are you feeling?'

'Not so bad,' he smiled, then winced. 'I'm not sure I'd tell you if I found another lump growing,' he warned me.

I was about to ask whether he wanted me to get him anything from the hospital shop, when the twin rubber doors to the unit flew open and Dr Kibble-White fell into the room. He was carrying a huge load of disposable equipment and tripped with practised ease on nothing in particular. He was in charge of the intensive care unit and clearly felt that his duties included keeping the supply cupboard well stocked.

Behind him came Hector, carrying an even larger bundle of catheters, disposable gloves, medicated swabs, drip sets, plastic syringes, sterilised needles and cotton wool. Hector stepped neatly over the anaesthetist's supine form, put his pile of goods down on Mr Kendall's bed and started to pick up Dr Kibble-White's load. I jumped up to help him.

'Thanks, lads,' said Dr Kibble-White cheerily. He examined his stethoscope to make sure it wasn't damaged, and straightened his white coat.

'Are you all right?' asked Sister Yardley solicitously. 'Do you need anything?'

'Fine, thanks, Lizzie,' answered the anaesthetist. He was the only doctor in the hospital who dared to call Sister Yardley by her Christian name. She seemed to like it. The two of them disappeared into the tiny office, while Hector and I carried on sorting out the confusion on the floor.

'What are you doing here?' he asked, examining a drip set that had burst through its plastic packaging and would therefore have to be thrown away.

'Seeing Mr Kendall.'

'I thought you were doing dermatology this week?'

'I am, but one of the patients turned out to have an aneurysm in his groin. Mr Meridew's just operated on him.'

'I'm doing a fortnight's anaesthetics,' said Hector. 'It isn't officially in the curriculum, but Mr Knibb thought it might be useful for me, so he had a word with Dr Kibble-White and Professor Grainger.'

He was explaining to me how Mr Knibb has suggested that a little basic experience in anaesthetics would prove very vital for anyone contemplating a surgical career, when Dr Kibble-White emerged from the office.

'Right! Let's have a look round,' he said, clapping his hands together sharply.

I jumped. Then we began the impromptu ward-round, with a man in his mid-thirties.

'This is Mr Shipton,' said Dr Kibble-White.

'Shipley,' corrected the patient.

'Dreadfully sorry. Shipley,' said the anaesthetist, leaning forward and patting the patient on the forearm. He winced; Kibble-White's pat was more like anyone else's smack. 'Mr Shipley came into the hospital last Tuesday.'

'Wednesday,' said the patient.

'Sorry. Wednesday... He's thirty-eight-years-old.'

'Thirty-seven.'

Dr Kibble-White sighed. 'This young man came in last week,' he said quickly, 'complaining of palpitations. He told us that several times he'd noticed his heart taking an extra beat or two.' He looked with a raised eyebrow at Mr Shipley.

'Is that all right?'

Mr Shipley nodded. He looked very earnest as I suppose he had every right to do. It was, after all, his body Dr Kibble-White was discussing.

'Tell us about the first time,' said Dr Kibble-White encouragingly.

'My brother and I had decided to go to Newbury Races for the day,' said Mr Shipley. 'There was a horse running in the 3.30 that Fred thought stood a good chance.' He paused and looked at the anaesthetist who nodded encouragement. 'To be honest,' he said, 'he'd had a good tip about it.'

'Did it win?' asked Dr Kibble-White.

Mr Shipley shook his head. 'No,' he said sadly, 'but we won on a young horse in the four o'clock. Just by a nose. Won us ten quid, though.'

'Did you have much to drink?'

'No. My brother drove us both down there, so he wasn't drinking. He got disqualified a few years ago and he's always been pretty careful since then. I don't like drinking when he can't. It isn't fair, is it?'

'No,' agreed Dr Kibble-White. 'Very sensible.'

'We got back home at about eight. Is that what you wanted to know?'

'Where did you eat?'

'We had some sandwiches my wife had put up for us.'

'And nothing exciting happened?'

'We didn't have any big win, if that's what you mean.'

'And yet that evening you had the first palpitations?'

'That's right. When I got home. I was sitting watching the television when they came. I thought I was going to die.'

'And how many times since then have you had them?'

'Twice. Once last week when I went to the cinema. I go with my brother once a month. He's divorced, you know, and gets a bit lonely now and then.'

'Just the two of you went?'

'That's right.'

'Did you have anything to drink?'

Mr Shipley shook his head.

'And nothing particularly exciting happened that day?'

Again Mr Shipley shook his head.

'Where did you eat?'

'At home before we went out.'

'And when did you get the palpitations?'

'Towards the end of the big feature. I thought I was going to die.'

'What happened on the third occasion?'

'We were repairing our garage doors. They've been sticking for months and I decided to try to take them off and oil them.'

'Hard work?'

'Not particularly.'

'Did you have any help?'

'My brother came and helped me out.'

'And after that you had some extra heartbeats again?'

Mr Shipley nodded.

'Right,' said Dr Kibble-White. 'You now have all the information you need, gentlemen, to make a diagnosis. We've had Mr Shipton on the unit here for several days and we haven't found anything wrong with him at all. He hasn't had any extra beats since he's been in the hospital and he's got no other symptoms at all.'

'Shipley,' said the patient quietly.

'Shipley,' corrected Dr Kibble-White. 'I beg your pardon.'

'Not alcohol?' said Hector.

Dr Kibble-White shook his head. 'You heard the story.'

'And not physical exercise?'

Dr Kibble-White shook his head again.

'They were extra-systoles?' I suggested. 'A pause and then a strong beat?'

'Certainly sounded like that,' agreed Dr Kibble-White, 'and that's what we decided. We got Professor Grainger to look at him after he was admitted here and that's what he decided as well.'

'Once after he went to the races,' said Hector, counting on his fingers, 'once after a visit to the cinema...'

'During a visit to the cinema,' Dr Kibble-White corrected him.

'...during a visit to the cinema, and thirdly after repairing the garage doors.'

'I can't see any connection,' I said.

'I take it there is a connection?' said Hector.

'There is,' agreed Dr Kibble-White. 'His brother was with him on each occasion. Right, Mr Shipley?'

Mr Shipley nodded.

'He can't be allergic to his brother, surely,' said Hector.

Dr Kibble-White shook his head.

Hector and I looked at each other and shrugged.

'I give up,' I said finally.

'Me, too,' agreed Hector.

'Do you smoke, Mr Shipton?' asked Dr Kibble-White.

Mr Shipley, ignoring the mistake this time, nodded.

'How many a day?'

'Ten or so.'

'Always?'

Mr Shipley shook his head. 'Occasionally I smoke more.'

'When?' asked Dr Kibble-White.

'When I'm being sociable,' said the patient. 'My brother smokes a lot and I always smoke more when I'm with him.'

'There you are!' said Dr Kibble-White triumphantly. 'Mr Shipton gets extra-systoles when he smokes too many cigarettes. The connection between tobacco and extra systoles is quite well-known.'

'Of course,' said Hector and I meekly.

The next patient, an elderly but still attractive woman whose bed was surrounded by screens to provide her with some modesty, beamed at Dr Kibble-White and held out her hand to him. To her apparent delight, he kissed it instead of shaking it.

'This is Mrs Turner,' he said. 'She was admitted for investigations when she began to complain of chest pains three days ago.'

Hector and I said hello to her.

'She only gets chest pains when she goes to the lavatory,' said Dr Kibble-White. 'Isn't that so, Mrs Turner?' Mrs Turner nodded.

'Why do you think that might be?' asked the anaesthetist.

'Do you get short of breath?' asked Hector.

She shook her head. 'Not a lot.'

'Do you get the pain before you've used the lavatory, while you're using it or after you've used it?' asked Hector.

'It varies. Sometimes before, sometimes during and sometimes afterwards.'

That really puzzled us. There are pains which can occur at specific times when related to visits to the lavatory, but neither Hector nor I could think of anything likely to cause pain in such a vague way.

'Tell them where your lavatory is,' said Dr Kibble-White.

'Down the yard,' said Mrs Turner.

'So if it's chilly you have to go out into the cold to get there?'

She nodded.

'Any idea, gentlemen?' Dr Kibble-White asked us.

'Angina?' We both suggested at once.

'Absolutely. Mrs Turner gets angina when she goes out into the cold.'

Mrs Turner nodded and beamed at us both.

'So what's the treatment?' asked Dr Kibble-White.

'Glyceryl trinitrate?' suggested Hector.

Dr Kibble-White shook his head. 'Have an indoor lavatory built.'

With that he moved on to Mr Kendall, who grinned at me and winked.

'Hello, Mr Kendall,' said the anaesthetist. Mr Kendall shook his outstretched hand.

'How are you?'

'Not too bad,' said Mr Kendall. 'But it's come back.'

Both Dr Kibble-White and I, who knew how big the aneurysm had been, were startled when we heard that.

'When?' asked Dr Kibble-White.

'An hour or so ago.'

Dr Kibble-White yanked back the bedclothes. We all peered at Mr Kendall's right groin where a huge mountain of bandages and padding hid the wound that marked the site of his aneurysm.

'Not that,' he said, as Dr Kibble-White pressed it gently.

'What, then?' asked the anaesthetist puzzled.

'My rash. That's what I came in with originally.'

Sure enough his abdomen was covered with a fine red rash.

'Why's it come back now?' he asked. 'I thought it had gone for good.'

Both Hector and I stared at the anaesthetist and waited.

'That just goes to show you that in medicine you must always be prepared for the unexpected,' he said. 'And,' he added, pulling the bedclothes back and moving away from the bed, 'always ready to ask for help when you have no idea of the diagnosis.' He grinned at us both and disappeared, stumbling out through the twin rubber doors and colliding with a porter wheeling a trolley in the corridor.

Chapter Twenty Eight

When my week in the skin department was over I found myself allocated to the rheumatology clinic where Dr Underhill, one of the oldest physicians in the hospital, was in charge. He was a delightful gentleman who lived in an enormous country house twenty miles away from St Peter's. He commuted to work each day in an ancient but immaculate Rolls-Royce. Although he'd once defined an expert as a man with slides and a speech impediment who travels a long way to bore people, Dr Underhill was an inveterate speaker whose failing memory caused him innumerable problems. There was even a celebrated story of his being rescued from a small Spanish airport in his carpet slippers without either money or passport. Despite this, his clinical acumen was astonishingly sharp, and even Dr Kibble-White's deductive skills seemed ordinary in comparison. I can still remember vividly my first morning in his clinic.

Held in a room which had formerly been a recreation hall, it was more like a social event than anything else. Dr Underhill sat in an ancient leather chair, kept especially for him, at an extremely old and battered wooden desk containing numerous small drawers, each stocked with a supply of different forms. The rest of the hall had long since been equipped with modern tubular-steel furniture, but Dr Underhill refused to have anything to do with such monstrosities. The administrative staff had several times attempted to force his hand, but every time he'd won, and retained his right to sit on a chair he liked at a desk he found functional and comfortable.

Around him sat the patients on their uncomfortable modern chairs, waiting patiently for the great man to work his way through the clinic. The patient being examined sat on a chair on the other side of Dr Underhill's desk and the two of them, together with any medical students present, were in full view of all the other patients. If a patient needed to be examined physically he'd be allowed to go behind a screen. Dr Underhill insisted that this system allowed the waiting patients to see just why they were having to wait, and that it also gave them a certain amount of entertainment; certainly no one ever complained about it while I was at St Peter's, and no patients ever seemed to read magazines or books while waiting.

Although the clinic was described as the 'rheumatology clinic', it wasn't anything of the kind in practice. Dr Underhill's diagnostic skills were so well respected that general practitioners and even other consultants who had difficult diagnostic problems would often send their patients along to be seen by the great man.

'Now then, doctors,' Dr Underhill began as Andrew and I sat down with him, 'let's see what we've got today.' He picked up a small brass bell on his desk and rang it gently.

Since all the patients could see him and they all sat in order of their arrival at the clinic, there was no need for a complex system of communication.

The first patient lumbered forward and sat down. He was a young man with acne bursting through his aftershave lotion and greasy hair hanging over his collar.

'What is your name, sir?' asked Dr Underhill politely.

'Howell,' said the patient. He was rather surly and sharp.

'And your Christian name?'

'Robert.'

'Where do you live, Mr Howell?'

'Nugent Road.'

'The Westlea Avenue end?'

'No, the Kennington Road end.'

'So you're near the Black Bear?' said Dr Underhill whose knowledge of the area around St Peter's was legendary.

Mr Howell nodded.

'Is Mr Lazenby still the landlord there?'

'Yes, Doctor.' The patient was beginning to thaw a little. He hadn't expected to find a physician who knew so much about his home ground.

'Do you know Nugent Road?' Dr Underhill asked Andrew and me.

We both shook our heads.

'Very interesting part of the country. There used to be a private zoo there fifty or sixty years ago. The motor taxation offices now stand where the lions' den used to be.' He smiled. 'Very apt.'

'I didn't know that,' said Mr Howell.

'And Mr Busby, the gentleman who owned the zoo, ran a woodyard halfway along Kennington Road. It was burnt down during the Second World War and they built a motor components factory on the site.'

'That's where my dad works,' said Mr Howell, astonished.

'Splendid,' said Dr Underhill, nodding approval.

'I work at Simpson's, the garage on the corner of Nugent Road and Kennington Road,' said Mr Howell, offering information freely for the first time.

'Have either of you gentlemen ever worked in a garage?'

Dr Underhill asked us.

We shook our heads again.

'Fascinating places. There's something magnificent about a good piece of machinery. And there's intense satisfaction to be derived from repairing a fault in one. Is that not so, Mr Howell?'

Mr Howell, who by this time would have confirmed that the earth is flat and made of meringue if Dr Underhill had suggested it, agreed wholeheartedly.

'You young doctors should learn more about the work your patients do,' Dr Underhill told us. 'Still, I suppose these days you don't get time to interest yourself in things like that.' He shook his head slowly from side to side. 'Very sad.'

'I think you're very right on that point, sir,' said Andrew. 'I'd like to have the chance to see a bit more of the environment in which my patients are working.'

Dr Underhill raised an eyebrow and nodded twice.

'I think we get too much to learn. Too much fact and not enough opportunity to learn a little wisdom,' continued Andrew.

'That's not a viewpoint likely to endear you to the Dean,' Dr Underhill warned him. 'But I must say it's one I believe in myself. I rather feel there's too much emphasis these days on modern forms of diagnosis and therapy.' He pushed his fingers together so that his hands formed a steeple, and rested his chin on his fingertips.

'Of course,' he went on, 'my views are rather heretical, and you mustn't take them too seriously.' He sighed. 'But, for what it's worth, I do rather think that any condition for which there is a host of cures is rather likely to be incurable.' He paused again and nodded to himself thoughtfully. Then he turned to Mr Howell. 'You must think us very opinionated,' he said, 'but I do believe that false modesty is the prerogative of the minimally talented.'

Mr Howell smiled weakly.

'My dad always wanted me to go to university,' he said unexpectedly. 'But I wanted to get married.'

'Are you married, Mr Howell?'

'No. She left me to marry a bank clerk. She thought he had better prospects. Probably right, too.'

'Ah.'

'Do you really not believe in modern methods of treatment?' asked Andrew.

'I don't think that's quite what I said,' Dr Underhill corrected him carefully. 'What I did hope to imply was that much modern medicine is based on unnecessary technology. And many so-called modern discoveries are merely resurrections of existing information which has been temporarily mislaid. I don't have too much faith in modern researchers. At least, not as much as some of my colleagues.'

I couldn't help thinking that in spite of his reputation for a poor memory Dr Underhill seemed sharp enough. When he wanted to remember things, he seemed to manage well enough.

He went on to tell us that five thousand years ago the Egyptians used opiates for surgical patients and used alcohol as an antiseptic. They splinted broken bones and had sticking plasters for minor cuts and abrasions. They even used dream and music therapy, and could provide patients with artificial limbs and eyes.

‘An Egyptian doctor who tried out a new treatment which failed forfeited his life,’ he told us, raising both eyebrows and looking at each of us in turn. ‘There are a few physicians around today who might think twice if such rules were reintroduced.’

‘Absolutely,’ said Andrew enthusiastically. I wondered if Dr Underhill had heard about Andrew’s troubles and was trying, in a roundabout way, to let him know that his accusations weren’t entirely without support.

He told us that four thousand years ago in India operating-theatres were purified with fragrant smoke, sheets were cleaned with steam and surgical instruments boiled before being used. Hospitals were, he said, filled with peaceful music, perfume and flowers and decorated with bright colours. Surgeons had to keep their hands scrubbed, wear clean white clothes, keep their nails short and their mouths shut when they operated. The ancient Indians, he claimed, knew that germs can be carried on the breath.

He explained that the Greeks used heat, exercise and massage to relieve pain. ‘The Greek women,’ he said, ‘even used intra-uterine contraceptive devices.’

Some of the patients waiting to see him dragged their chairs forward an inch or two so as to hear better. Dr Underhill’s impromptu dissertations were famous, and many television producers and chat-show hosts had tried to persuade him to repeat them for a larger audience. They’d always failed.

‘Two thousand years ago Dioscorides described digitalis, and an Arabian physician called Rhazes, who was looking for sites to build hospitals, hung pieces of meat in various likely spots, then chose the places where the meat had lasted the longest.’ Dr Underhill shrugged his shoulders. ‘We still use digitalis. It’s one of the most important drugs we have. And we could do worse than follow the Arab’s example when building our hospitals.’

‘Brain operations were performed thousands of years ago, and the Egyptians used penicillin four thousand years before Fleming found it. Blood transfusions and artificial teeth are centuries old and yet we make a great fuss of the people who reintroduced them.

'There's not much new,' he said sadly. 'And most of the stuff that is really new is unlikely ever to be of much use to those of us involved in practical medicine.' He leant back suddenly, put his hands flat on the desk and smiled straight at Mr Howell.

'I must apologise,' he said. 'I've undoubtedly been boring you.'

All three of us murmured our encouragement for him to continue, but he was adamant.

'Which of your relatives is diabetic?' he suddenly asked Mr Howell.

'My father and his brother,' replied the patient, rather surprised.

'When diabetes occurs in young people,' he explained, 'there's very often a family history of the disease.'

Neither of us had the faintest idea how he'd made the diagnosis. We just looked at him open-mouthed.

'Take this form to the laboratory.' Dr Underhill handed Mr Howell a piece of paper. 'They'll take a sample of your blood. Come back and see me in two hours' time.'

While Mr Howell made his way towards a large green and white sign which advertised the laboratory, Andrew and I, both desperate to learn how our mentor had made his diagnosis, began to speak at once.

'He had several large boils on his neck,' said Dr Underhill without waiting for either of us. 'And boils commonly occur in diabetics.'

'Was that enough to give you the diagnosis?' asked Andrew incredulously.

Dr Underhill shook his head. 'He'd also lost a good deal of weight. His clothes were far too big for him, and people whose jobs are messy usually dress well when they're not at work.' He smiled at us. 'I'm sure you know that diabetics often lose weight before they're diagnosed.'

We both nodded.

'Finally, I have to confess that when Mr Howell approached my desk I noticed white powdery stains on the insides of both of his shoes and on the lower part of his right trouser leg.'

It meant nothing to either of us. I was beginning to doubt if I could ever become even an adequate diagnostician.

Andrew must have been feeling the same. 'What did that show?'

'Sugar. Dried sugar. His urine is so loaded with sugar that the drops that fell on his shoes and trousers dried to leave sugary stains there.'

While Andrew and I stared at him with awe, Dr Underhill reached out and gently rang his small brass bell.

I sat with him in his clinic several times after that, and each time I learnt a tremendous amount about life, history, and the art of making a diagnosis without asking too many unnecessary questions. He was a marvellous man and, when his retirement came a few months later, thousands of his patients clubbed together to buy him a solid silver salver. In addition there were not a few contributions from his former students.

Chapter Twenty Nine

The weeks were disappearing far too quickly. The medical student of half a century ago, even of two decades ago, had much less information to cope with. Today there's not only basic anatomy and physiology; he must also know something about biochemistry, physics, engineering and computer programming. Books on paediatrics, gynaecology, surgery, obstetrics, pharmacology, orthopaedics, pathology, psychiatry, dermatology, ophthalmology, cardiology, rheumatology, haematology, gastro-enterology and even sociology have to be read. At the same time, there are ward-rounds to attend and patients to examine. In addition, the unfortunate student has to come to terms with the fact that much of what he learns will, by the time he qualifies, be out-of-date, and more will soon become so.

Meanwhile the available information must be prepared for reproduction when required. We didn't simply have to face a single major examination at the end of our studies. Along the way we were watched by our teachers and professors, and the results of their observations helped to decide whether or not we'd qualify. At any time I had to be aware that a casually asked but incorrectly answered question might well lead to a black mark against my name. And there were still the final examinations, too. The last few months of a medical education are 'stress-rich', and it's no wonder that so many students crack under the pressure and need medical help themselves.

As the final days approached, Andrew, Hector and I found ourselves joining Professor Grainger's ward-rounds as often as we could. Officially there was no longer any need for us to attend rounds at all. But we all agreed that much of medicine can't be learnt from books; solid practical experience is irreplaceable. Besides, we half-hoped that the patients who'd appear in our final examinations might come from among those in the Professor's hospital beds. It was, of course, an entirely fruitless hope; patients for examinations are always brought in specially, like poor old Mrs Kennedy.

Unfortunately, Professor Grainger's rounds weren't

always as captivating as they might have been. It was after two unusually dreary sessions, during which we'd been subjected to an exceptionally long harangue about the iniquities of socialised medicine, that Andrew and I had an idea for adding a little extra spice to the procedure. We decided to run a sweepstake on the time taken for Professor Grainger to complete his morning round. It was best, we felt, to time it from the moment when he said 'Good morning' to Sister Henderson on the female medical ward, where he always began, to the moment when he said 'Goodbye' to Sister Wills on the male medical ward.

Originally we'd intended to confine the sweepstake to the students directly involved, but the idea quickly spread, and within two days more than seventy people had paid a pound and chosen the time for which they thought the round would last. Since Professor Grainger had been known to take anything from ninety minutes to three or four hours, there was plenty of opportunity for them to select different times. There were some who chose arbitrarily, and others who used more scientific approaches, checking with both ward sisters on the patients likely to attract the Professor's attention. As instigator of the event I had a slight advantage, having timed each round for a fortnight. I worked out the average length and put that down as my estimated time.

There were twenty-seven patients on the female medical ward and on the day chosen for the sweepstake, Professor Grainger had seen no less than nine of them in the first ten minutes. While Andrew and I walked as slowly as we could, he forged ahead. Andrew was in charge of the stopwatch and every half-minute or so he took it out of his coat pocket and stared at it in astonishment. The other students, none of whom had chosen a time as short as the one the Professor seemed likely to take, straggled between him and us like out-of-condition runners.

We decided that we'd have to slow him down a little, and Andrew and I were busily whispering together to try to think of questions likely to trigger off a monologue of some substance, when he stopped at the end of the bed occupied by a woman who'd been admitted only that morning.

'Have a look at this patient,' he said to me, 'and tell me whether or not you'd pass her fit for driving a motor-car.'

I looked at him without understanding.

'One of the jobs of a medical adviser,' he explained with unexpected patience, 'is to adjudicate on problems such as this. To decide whether or not his patients are fit to have children, drive motor-cars or fly aeroplanes. This is Mr Vernon,' he said to his patient as I approached her bed. 'And this,' he added, speaking to me, 'is Mrs Bennett.'

Mrs Bennett and I smiled at each other, and I picked up her hand to feel her pulse. I wasn't at all sure how to begin the examination but I thought it might be a good idea to make sure her heart was beating.

'Tell me,' said Professor Grainger rather drily, 'exactly what sort of thing are you looking for?'

'Well, I want to make sure she isn't going to have a heart attack while driving.'

'Can you do that?' he asked incredulously. 'Can you really tell which patients are going to have heart attacks?'

'Well, not exactly,' I admitted.

'Of course you can't. If you could, you'd be able to make a fortune working for the insurance companies. All you can do is quote the odds.'

'Well, her pulse is fine,' I told him. 'Regular, seventy and of good volume.'

'I'm sure Mrs Bennett will be pleased to hear that,' he said — rather sarcastically, I thought. 'What else do you think you should check on?'

'To make sure she's got full use of her limbs.'

'And how are you going to do that?'

'I'll test her reflexes and muscle power and look at her sensory system.'

'We don't have that much time,' said the Professor. 'Can't you think of a quicker way to make sure she's got limbs that work?'

By this time he'd got me thoroughly confused.

'In a few weeks' time,' he said, 'you may well be a doctor. It's hard to believe, but it seems possible. How would you check to see that this woman can move her limbs?'

'I could see if she walks all right,' I suggested.

'Splendid!' he said with a broad and artificial smile.

I asked Mrs Bennett to get out of bed and watched while she walked a few yards up the ward.

'That's fine,' I said.

'You're happy with her legs, Mr Vernon?'

I nodded.

'And what about her arms?'

'They seem fine.'

'Try them out!' he shouted. 'You don't have to dance with her, but check out her arms. Make sure her coordination is good.'

I took out my patella-hammer, but the professor was clearly not prepared to wait for such niceties.

'Catch!' he said suddenly to Mrs Bennett, picking an apple out of her fruit-bowl and throwing it to her. She caught it neatly. 'Seems all right to me,' he commented. He looked around and everyone murmured agreement.

'Right,' he said. 'Now you've tested her limbs and her heart. What else?'

'Her eyes?'

'Very good, Mr Vernon.'

I picked up the newspaper which lay on her bed and held it up. 'Can you read this?'

She read out a couple of news items without any difficulty.

'So what's your decision?' asked Professor Grainger. 'Do you think she's fit to drive?'

'Yes.'

'Pity. You're wrong.' He turned to Mrs Bennett. 'Would you say you were fit to drive a motor-car?' She shook her head and looked at me as if asking me to forgive her. I smiled at her.

'Test her visual fields,' the Professor told me.

I looked straight at her and asked her to close one eye. Then I started moving my fingers around first on the left and then on the right. I asked her to tell me when she could see them. It quickly became clear that, although her sight directly in front of her was quite good, she couldn't see anything either to the right or to the left. She was like a horse wearing blinkers.

'That is called tunnel vision, Mr Vernon,' said the Professor, 'and I think you'll agree that Mrs Bennett would be a hazard on the roads. Goodbye for now, Mrs Bennett. We'll try to find out during the next few days exactly what's causing your problem.' He smiled at her and patted her hand.

Then we moved on to the next patient. Andrew pointed to his stopwatch. The round had been in progress for nearly forty-five minutes.

We spent ten minutes discussing the various possible causes of headache in a forty-two-year-old woman before coming to the communal conclusion that the problem was probably caused by a tumour of some kind. Only then did Professor Grainger tell us that when drunk her husband had hit her with a milk-bottle.

We stood, watched and listened for twelve minutes while the professor examined a twenty-three-year-old shop assistant with the staring eyes and swollen neck typical of thyrotoxicosis, and we all examined a lump in a thirty-eight-year-old woman's groin: it turned out to be a young hernia which ought to have been investigated on a surgical ward. That took another seventeen minutes.

The last bed was occupied by a Miss Rogers, according to the label attached to her bedside locker. The screens were pulled around her so that she was quite invisible.

'What's wrong with Miss Rogers?' asked Professor Grainger after studying his watch carefully.

'She's got a pleural effusion,' said Dr Taylor, his registrar, studying the case-notes which Sister Henderson had handed to him.

'Right,' said the Professor. 'Then, let's have a look.' Ignoring a stifled cry of warning from the sister he flung back the screens. It wasn't the wisest thing he could have done, for the poor woman was sitting perched uncomfortably on a bedpan, and her cries of dismay were far from stifled. She struggled to hide herself, but dignity's impossible in such a situation and she only made things worse. Mumbling apologies, Professor Grainger redrew the curtains and we all hurried off. The tour of the female medical ward had occupied a total of just over one and a half hours.

The first patient to be examined on the male medical ward was a boy of eleven with Gilles de la Tourette syndrome. This extraordinary disease, also known as compulsive coprolalia, is manifested in an unusual way. The sufferer simply shouts out obscenities for no apparent reason and at the top of his voice. It was for this excellent reason that the patient was here rather than on a children's ward. The poor young fellow's physical tics could be ignored. His verbal indecencies could not. Even on an adult ward, the effect on the other patients was such that some gnashed their teeth, while even the edentulous ones rubbed their gums together.

'Good morning, Roger,' said Professor Grainger, bending forward. 'How are you?'

'Fuck!' screamed young Roger, throwing his head to one side and grimacing.

'This is a nice motor-car,' said the Professor, picking up a small toy which was standing on Roger's locker.

'Shit!' shouted Roger, smiling broadly. 'Fuck!' he added after a moment.

It was difficult to imagine that these obscene utterances resulted entirely from a mental disorder. And important to remember. Professor Grainger tried for several minutes to begin a sensible conversation, but he was entirely unsuccessful.

'Pity that he wasn't in here when we had Mr Blake with us,' I heard the Professor whisper as we moved on to the next patient.

He saw the next seven patients in four minutes. I realised that my chance of winning the sweepstake was slim. The other patients in the male ward were all suffering from diseases which seemed positively mundane after poor Roger.

Andrew made a brave attempt to slow down the

proceedings by introducing into the conversation the name of one of Professor Grainger's arch-rivals — a professor at another teaching hospital who'd written papers on several of the subjects Professor Grainger considered his own province. But with the stopwatch showing one hour and fifty-five minutes the Professor said goodbye to Sister Wills and waved cheerfully to the rest of us.

Once he'd disappeared, Andrew produced from his pocket the seventy slips of paper upon which were written the names of the sweepstake ticket-holders together with their estimated times. He refused to show them to anyone until we had all adjourned to the staff restaurant. Then he ceremoniously placed them on the table, one by one. Only one bore the right time, and when we read the name of the person who'd 'guessed' it no one spoke for several minutes.

The winner was Professor Grainger himself.

Chapter Thirty

Suddenly the weeks, months and years of preparation were all over. The final examination was upon us and there were no more chances to hide our ignorance. It included two written papers and several practical tests. The written parts were relatively straightforward, although they did demand the ability not only to retain knowledge but also to reproduce it. And, since doctors-to-be inevitably have illegible handwriting, it did demand a certain amount of patience on the part of both students and examiners. There were rumours that, in the past, teams of pharmacists had been brought in to help examiners decipher particularly bad cases.

The practical tests were far less predictable. There were several patients to be seen, and the examiners, who included Professor Grainger and an external examiner from another medical school, hovered in the background to make sure that the examination itself was conducted properly. It wasn't enough simply to find the right diagnosis.

We waited for this in the corridor outside the medical wards, and in a small room usually used by patients' relatives. It was so cold there that every time the door opened I expected the light to come on. I found myself standing with two other students, whom I knew only slightly despite the fact that all three of us were in the same batch. Conversation was non-existent, since we all stood reciting mnemonics and phrases designed to help us solve diagnostic puzzles.

Eventually I found myself sitting by the bedside of a woman aged about fifty. She wore a revealing black nightdress and her lips and fingernails were coated with bright red cosmetics. I introduced myself and asked her name.

'Deirdre,' she said, staring at me rather oddly. 'Deirdre Jackson.'

'Are you married?' I asked.

'I was.' And then quite unexpectedly she burst into tears. That nearly threw me off completely; when you're examining the most important patient of your life you don't want her to start crying almost before you've sat down.

'I buried him three months ago,' she told me, taking the handkerchief I offered her. Her speech was slurred and difficult to follow.

'What was wrong with him?'

'He was dead.'

I closed my eyes and I began to pray. At that moment I honestly couldn't see how I was ever going to produce a diagnosis for this woman.

'He was awful to me,' she said. As suddenly as she'd started she stopped crying and handed me back the handkerchief. 'I did everything for him,' she added. I wondered if she was drunk.

'I'm sure you did,' I agreed, hoping that I could somehow persuade her to start answering some specific questions.

'I used to work every night while he just went out drinking. And I spent two hundred pounds buying him a set of golf clubs.'

I couldn't smell any alcohol — and where would she get it in hospital?

'How old are you, Mrs Jackson?'

'He just said I'd bought them for him so that he'd go off and play golf and leave me to my lovers.'

I couldn't think of anything to say to that.

'It wasn't true. I didn't have any lovers. I was faithful to him.'

'I'm sure you were,' I said, still hoping that by agreeing with her I could win her over.

'You're very nice,' she said, putting her hand out and on top of mine. Out of the corner of my eye I could see Professor Grainger and Professor Yarborough, the visiting examiner.

Professor Yarborough was also a member of the General Medical Council, and I wondered if anyone had ever been struck off the register before they'd actually qualified.

'But you won't be able to keep it up,' she said sadly.

I tried to move my hand away.

'Oh dear,' she giggled. 'What have I said? I laid myself

wide open then, didn't I?' She moved over in the bed so that her head was closer to me. 'Do what you want with me,' she whispered.

I moved back sharply, sweat pouring off my forehead.

'I'm a dreadful person,' she said suddenly starting to cry again. 'I've always been causing trouble. I'm just not worth keeping alive. Why don't you have me put to sleep?'

'Do you ever get short of breath?' I asked her. I was desperate to try to restore some resemblance of sense to the examination. I had thirty minutes in which to make a diagnosis and so far I'd used up nearly half of that and got absolutely nowhere.

'I lied to you,' she said unexpectedly. Everything about her was unpredictable. 'My husband isn't dead. He left me.'

'When did he leave you?'

'I can't remember.'

'Why did he leave you?'

She just looked at me and said nothing.

'How old are you?' I asked again.

'Thirty-three,' she said. 'I think.' She frowned, thinking.

'Do you have any pains?'

'D'you think I'm going to die?'

'Why do you ask that?'

'I'm going to die, aren't I?'

'Do you feel ill?'

'I'm dying, aren't I?'

'Why do you ask that, Mrs Jackson?'

But Mrs Jackson wasn't answering any questions. She just began to cry again.

'Hold out your hands,' I told her. I wanted to have a look at her and see if I could find any clues. There wasn't much to see. Her fingernails were painted a vivid red, and the nail varnish had been applied crudely, with splashes of it on her skin. I noticed that when she held her hands out they were trembling slightly.

'Right, then, Mr Vernon,' said a voice very quietly behind me. 'Would you like to come with us?' It was Professor Grainger. I stared at him horrified.

'Your time's up,' he told me. 'Would you come with us

so that we can ask you about Mrs Jackson?'

Muttering my thanks to Mrs Jackson, although I wasn't quite sure what for, I followed the Professor down the ward to a small area that had been screened off. There were three chairs there; the two examiners sat down, pointing to the third chair for me.

'Well,' said Professor Yarborough. 'What did you think of her?'

'I'm afraid I didn't get very much from her,' I admitted, dazed. What on earth had been wrong with the damned woman? Why hadn't she been a bit more co-operative?

'Well, do you think that was your fault or her fault?' asked Professor Grainger quietly. I was astonished to see how gentle he could be.

'I think she was confused.'

'Did she say anything sensible?'

'No,' I said, more confidently now. 'She was rather demented.' I was astonished. Of course, that was why I hadn't been able to get anything sensible out of her. She was demented!

'Fine,' said Professor Grainger, smiling at me. 'Fine.'

I wondered if he was deliberately leading me off course.

'She seemed depressed and paranoid,' I went on. 'And frightened that she was dying.'

Professor Grainger nodded encouragement. Professor Yarborough was picking at his thumbnail.

'She made a sort of crude sexual advance,' I said, blushing.

'Do all patients do that to you?'

'No!' I said quickly.

'So that may well be indicative of some specific aspect of her illness?'

I nodded.

'What else did you notice about her?'

'She had a slight tremor and her speech was slurred,' I told him. 'I did wonder if she was drunk.'

'But you knew that we wouldn't have let her drink on the ward.'

I nodded again.

‘What else did you notice?’ That was Professor Yarborough.

‘Her nail varnish was applied rather carelessly.’

‘Good,’ said Professor Grainger.

‘So what do you think the likely diagnosis is?’ asked Professor Yarborough.

‘I don’t know, sir,’ I admitted. It was getting bad again.

‘Do you know what her job was?’ I thought for a moment.

‘She said she’d been working at night to earn money,’ I remembered.

‘And what women work at night?’

‘Nurses?’

‘That’s a rather parochial view,’ smiled Professor Grainger.

‘If I asked a man on the street what sort of women worked at night, what do you think he’d say?’

‘Ladies of, er, easy virtue,’ I stammered.

‘Prostitutes!’

‘Prostitutes,’ I agreed.

‘So do you think that Mrs Jackson might have been a prostitute?’

‘Yes.’

On an ordinary ward-round I’d have expected him to make some comment about my assuming that all women who worked at night were prostitutes. But he didn’t.

‘Put together Mrs Jackson’s former occupation and her present condition and make a guess at the diagnosis.’

‘General Paralysis of the Insane?’ I suggested.

‘Absolutely,’ he said. ‘So what do you think the treatment should be?’

‘Penicillin.’

‘Good,’ he smiled. ‘And the prognosis? What do you think that is?’

‘Good?’

‘Well done!’ he told me. ‘Do you have any more questions?’ he asked Professor Yarborough.

‘I don’t think so,’ said Professor Yarborough, lifting his head for a moment to smile at me.

Realising that they'd finished with me, I lurched out of the ward.

Chapter Thirty One

The waiting after the examination was, if anything, even worse than the examination itself. A thousand times I went over everything I'd written and said. A thousand times I thought of things I could have said better or put more lucidly. A thousand times I thought about that dreadful interview with Mrs Jackson. What if they'd deliberately led me on to the wrong diagnosis? Perhaps they'd been letting me dig myself into a hole.

At least it lasted only two days. Unlike many other students, medical students don't have to suffer prolonged agonies while they wait for the examiners to make up their minds; largely perhaps because those who have in fact qualified are needed on the hospital wards.

I did much of my waiting at the local cricket ground. The weather was nice and warm — 'mainly dry with rain in places, sunny intervals and scattered showers' — and the cricket was probably good. But they might as well have been playing skittles in a thunderstorm. My mind was still on the wards. I remembered Mr and Mrs Kennedy, Ellen Richards and young Michael Jones. I thought about my first night in the casualty department three years before, and my stay at the Kintbury General. I reflected on my experiences in the operating-theatre and wondered how Mr Tucker was. And Mr Kendall, too.

Most of my fellow-students had already got jobs. All newly qualified medical students have to work for a year in hospital before being allowed to practise outside. There are six months as a house physician to be done, and six months as a house surgeon. Hector had his jobs all lined up — good ones in highly respected units. And even Andrew had his future neatly arranged. He'd marry Sara and move north. When she'd come back from Canada, Sara had, much to her father's disgust, still been determined. The wedding was fixed for a few weeks' time, and I was aware that I'd soon have to start preparing my speech.

I still had nothing planned, however. Until I'd seen my name on the noticeboard and I knew that I'd qualified, I couldn't start thinking about the future. There'd be plenty of places to work, plenty of chances to find a job. Perhaps I'd get a job at the Kintbury General if they had room.

I still wasn't even sure about my future in medicine. When I'd started at St Peter's I'd been filled with good intentions. My vocation had been for medicine, and nothing else had ever appealed to me. But somehow those five years had done something to my determination. I still found it difficult to control my feelings for the patients I looked after. I remembered them when I should have forgotten them, and I worried about them when I should have been worrying about their disorders.

The flat was filled with a mixture of gloom, despair and exhilaration. After the final day of our examinations we'd received three visits from men trying to sell us life insurance policies. They'd all been persuasive and we'd all been euphoric at having completed the examination, so we'd all bought policies we didn't really want or need. These were crazy days. Perhaps the last.

The day the results were due to be posted, I paced up and down in the drizzle, waiting for cries of excitement to tell me that the clerk had arrived armed with lists of names and two drawing-pins.

I knew I'd passed before I got anywhere near the noticeboard.

'Congratulations, Doctor!' shouted Hector. 'I'm Dr Melton.'

'Dr Vernon, I presume?' shouted someone else.

And there it was. My name on the noticeboard in between someone called Herbert Trumper and someone called June Wallace. (Who were they?) And there was Hector's name.

But Andrew wasn't on the list. He hadn't passed.

'We're going along to the bar for a drink!' shouted Hector. 'Coming?'

I shook my head, and shouted back to ask him if he'd seen Andrew. He shrugged and turned away.

Eventually I found Andrew back in the flat with Sara.

He'd sneaked out when he'd seen his name missing, and gone to see the Dean. He'd been convinced that there'd been a typing error.

'He said there was no mistake,' said Andrew. 'I've failed.'

He and Sara sat arm in arm in the kitchen comforting each other.

'Why?' I asked him. 'Have you any idea why?'

'That's what I wanted to know,' said Andrew. 'I asked him if it was because of that business over Mr Devlin. You remember that?'

I nodded.

'He said it wasn't. He said it was because of Sara.'

'Sara!'

He nodded. A tear started to run down his cheek. He brushed it away angrily.

'But why Sara?'

'She was a patient when I met her. The Dean said I could get into trouble for having a non-professional relationship with a patient. He said I could stay on and take my finals again next year, but they'd have to be convinced that Sara and I weren't still seeing each other.'

'That's crazy! They can't do that!'

'They have,' he said simply.

'But I could understand it if they'd thrown you out for that business over Mr Devlin,' I said. 'They were offended about that. But what has Sara and you got to do with your ability to practise medicine?'

'I think it's just an excuse. I don't think they'll ever pass me.'

'What are you going to do?'

'We're going away for a couple of days. Going to try to work things out. Decide what to do.'

'But did you pass the examination?'

'The Dean said it didn't matter whether I had or not. He said they could still fail me even if I had. He wouldn't tell me.'

'Could Sara's father have been in touch with them?'

Sara shook her head. 'He wouldn't do that.' She was crying. 'Not even he would do that.'

I helped Andrew pack and promised to send on his things

from his locker at the medical school. Then I walked to the station with them. When they'd gone I sat on a bench and just stared at the station clock. I was a doctor; I'd just qualified, and I didn't feel in the slightest bit happy. Where was the joy I ought to feel?

After a while I made my way back to school. There was an impromptu party going on in the restaurant at St Peter's. Several dozen students and their girlfriends, now doctors and their young ladies, were dancing and singing together. In a corner someone was crying with happiness; someone else was vomiting endlessly. Half a dozen people were carrying Hector around and threatening to throw him into a bath of cold water.

'My watch!' he shouted, struggling to get free.

They let him down for a moment; he took off his watch and with drunken deliberation put it in his pocket. 'There you are,' he shouted. 'Now do your worst.' He saw me and waved furiously until they picked him up and took him off to be ducked.

Someone bumped into me and spilt beer over my trousers. A nurse I didn't know who'd come to the party in her uniform put her arms round my neck and told me to dance with her.

Somehow, however, I just wasn't in the mood for the festivities. It was all something of an anticlimax. Being a doctor wasn't a bit like I'd thought it would be. I'd finally entered the green pastures; it felt more as if I'd just walked the plank.

Also by Edward Vernon PRACTICE MAKES PERFECT and PRACTISE WHAT YOU PREACH

"The funniest of the funny doctor books I have read for years" — *Richard Gordon*

"Delightfully and wittily written.... His descriptions of daunting receptionists, magazine-strewn waiting rooms and hypochondriacal patients will strike many familiar chords, but Dr Vernon is at his best when recounting his encounters in the surgery and at the bedside. For anyone needing to be entertained and at times moved, there could be no better prescription than one chapter of Practice Makes Perfect to be taken each night at bedtime." — *Liverpool Echo*

"Truthful, well-observed and consistently readable" — *Daily Telegraph*

"Most of his adventures are funny, some hilarious; but he has the good sense to leaven the comedy lump with some that are sad, some touching. All are written lightly, easily, entertainingly.

Dr Vernon is on to a good thing; we could do with some more." — *Oxford Times*

We hope you enjoyed this book. If so we would be grateful if you would post a favourable review on Amazon. Thank you.

Printed in Great Britain
by Amazon

50232431R00109